THE WHITE NEGRO
or
A SERIES OF LECTURES
ON THE
RACE PROBLEM

by Rev. M. W. Thornton, B. D.
Author, Lecturer, Orator, Minister, Composer of Poetic Gems,
Eec.
COPYRIGHTED, 1894

Original Publishing in BURLINGTON, IOWA:
CONRAD LUTZ PRINTING AND PUBLISHING CO.
1894

Republication of the original edition by Akirim Press
Publishing;
Book Cover Design, edits, complete table of contents,
additional commentary and editor's afterword
copyright © 2026 by Mirika Mayo Cornelius
All Rights Reserved
ISBN 978-1-946870-22-3

This Revised Annotated Edition includes Editor's Afterword
by Mirika Mayo Cornelius.
Editor's Notes are in italics and are signified with an asterisk*.
All newspaper articles are public domain and fair use, being
prior to 1905.

To the memory of my Loving Parents, two Brothers and two Sisters, this volume is affectionately inscribed, by

THE AUTHOR

REV. M. W. THORNTON, B. D.

CONTENTS

PREFACE.

In sending forth this little volume of essays it is with a faith that it will prove a blessing to many, because of the truths which it proclaims in behalf of a wronged race. I do not solicit or expect any human commendation, but hope the following collection of facts may be accepted in behalf of the Afro-American citizen.

To many sources does the writer feel himself under the greatest obligation, for references received.

Convinced of my duty to present the truth in this little volume, regardless of partisan issues, I have selected facts from all sources possible, that justice, and nothing but justice, shall be given.

Hence, in pursuing the following remarks, I pray and trust you may read from an unprejudiced stand point, and that your sentiment, with that of others, may ring out in the chorus of "An Honest Plea for the White Negro."

BIOGRAPHY.

The author of this sketch, M. W. Thornton, known as the boy orator and preacher, is a son of Joseph and Mirah Thornton, both having been slaves.

He was born Feb. 3, 1873, in the city of Mt. Pleasant, Iowa. His minor life, until he arrived at the age of fifteen years, was spent in school, when, by the removal of his parents to Des Moines, Iowa, he was also compelled to remove just in the prime of his school days, at which time he had entered high school.

By this move, he was deprived of completing a high school course; yet with the ambition of a statesman, and the often expressed desire of becoming educated and a true leader of his people, the position to labor to which he was forced for some time was his making; at the end of which time, with renewed zeal and energy, and by the providence of God, the position was opened for him at a commercial school, where for six months he had taken the Amanuensis course, then being but sixteen years old. With matured ideas for a boy of this age, and being a member of the A. M. E. Church for eleven years, being converted when but eight years of age, the impressions of his early Christian days, with the forebodings of the Gospel commands, persuaded and led him to enter Drake University to qualify himself for the ministry. June 16,

1892, he completed the theological course, then only nineteen years old.

From the fifteenth to the eighteenth year of his life, is a period of marked interest, and as he trusts, is a prophecy of better days in the future. When but sixteen years of age, he was met in a debate on the race problem, by an opponent who was Democratic in principle, and who fought bravely for his biased and prejudiced opinions, but at last was defeated.

On September 30, 1890, he delivered an oration in behalf of Home and Foreign Missions, at an assembly of the A. M. E. Missionary Society, which occupied thirty minutes, and greatly distinguished him as an orator in the minds of those who heard him.

On May 14, 1891, he was sent as a delegate to represent St. Paul A. M. E. Sunday School at the annual convention, held at Ottumwa, Iowa, and received first place on thought and composition, as is recorded in the minutes.

On November 10, 1891, while in attendance at a political meeting, he was called upon to make an opening speech for the occasion. Being unprepared, and having never made a political speech before, he made the attempt at all hazards, and the following is the comments of one of the leading papers of the city: "The first speaker introduced was Mr. M. W. Thornton, a bright looking young man, who spoke on the future of his race in America. He advocated close organization, union of effort and the selection of competent leaders as the method by which the race could reach the place of influence to which it is right¬ fully entitled. Mr. Thornton, although a young man and a political speaker of little experience, left a pleasing impression with the audience. His manner was modest, his use of language was good, and his arguments clear and sound."

On December 29, 1892, he took the honor of being the champion Afro-American orator in the state of Iowa, being awarded a gold medal, and contesting with opponents from five to seven years older in age and experience, he being but eighteen years old at the time. On January 1, 1892, he was elected Superintendent of St. Paul A. M. E. Sunday School, being a candidate against ex Superintendents and men of wide influence. His inaugural address for the occasion was of such a character that his greatest opponents called for a copy of the same to be published.

Mr. Thornton is a promising young man in the ministry, and has held some of the largest churches among his people. As a gospel speaker he is quite powerful and touching, and always commands a ready hearing from those who once hear him. And last, but not least, when he began the composition of this little volume which you now read, he was but eighteen years old.

C. C. CURLESS, A. M.

The White Negro.

I.

IS A title seldom applied, and the only published effort known of to the author for proving the Negroes relation to this term.

That this description is a right one, or that the writers idea of the subject be understood, we would therefore invite you to a farther consideration of the question under discussion.

The idea that I would wish to convey of this subject, may not be that which the reader thus far, and at the first sight will glean; but after tracing the author's line of argument very carefully I am in hopes that you may arrive at the same conclusion as I have.

All races are not white, and neither is the Negro the only dark race. Color is only skin deep at the best, and is no manifestation of inward principles. Virtue is the symbol of purity, and is likened not unto colors, but the whole human race. White is also a term of purity, and where ever such like purities exist, in reality they are as white as the fleecy flakes of the falling snow or the downy breast of the harmless dove.

The idea then that to be pure one must be white, is only a mistaken idea based upon a missinformed judgment. The true patriots of purity are just as numerous in the ranks of one race, according to their numbers and opportunities, as there are in the one race alone who is possessed with the supposed white skin and their superior advantages.

I say supposed white, because in reality there is no race that can be truthfully called white, and if I am to be challenged upon this assertion, I affirm that it must first be proven to me that there is such a human being that is as white as the brightest paper or the flakes of snow and secondly, is the brightest race of people the whitest object known to man?

Now when these questions have been properly aired I am satisfied that you with myself will say the race of people who say, they are white, are either mistaken or the linguists and artists are wrong in their understanding of this term.

Yet, which ever way you would have it, the truth is, that any people may become as white as the snow or fair as the sun if they will only apply themselves to the means. Now with all fairness, I ask you to show me any race that is more pure, or whiter than the scorned Negro, because of his color. There is none I can authoritively say. Our numbers posessed with corrupt principles are many it is true; but where oh! where is his brother man? lieing in the same road of corruption is the faint, but truthful reply.

The martyr for his country, the statesman for the people, or the saint for his religion, may be found among the supposed white in the persons of Abraham Lincoln, Summer or Wyckliff.

But, we too can proudly hold up before your gaze representatives black in color, yet, white at heart, as Crispus Attucks, Fred. Douglass and Bishop Allen.

Show me the women of virtue on the one side and I will produce you the women of purity on the other.

Oh no! Mr. Prejudice, beauty alone does not lie in the skins of the white races; for when it comes to color nothing is so beautiful as the coal black hotentot of Africa with his straight hair and flattened features or anything more charming to the eye than the loving Creoles of Florida, or the bewiching colored people of America.

Of the latter I can say that their charms of beauty are far surpassing to many of the others, and when we recall a few cases in which their beauty has played a conspicuous part, you with many others will then verify this as a fact.

But a few months ago, to my surprise, and yet it should not have been such to me, I read in one of our leading papers of a young Miss from one of the leading families in St. Paul, Minn., who as the result of her choice for life voluntarily eloped with her father's elevator man. Here was a young lady whose future in her own color bid fair, whose father was rich in money, houses and land, and whose hand would have been readily accepted by any number of her color, yet amid all this she refused, and accepted in their places, not wealth nor Caucasian, but the object of her love, which was all centered in her father's poor, but beautiful Negro.

Thus while we find that beauty is not found in the white race alone, I can say truthfully that it is found wherever purity may reign.

Is it not a fact, that all objects of adoration are not beautiful? yet such objects maybe ever so white or pure. One person admires another regardless of color and calls them white or pure; another admires another race and they are called loveable sometimes, while in looks they are every thing but that, and if you know not the reason of this I can tell you, it is because hidden in their heart and beaming eyes, and touching in every word they utter there is purity, there is the whiteness, there is the hidden beauty though hid by its rougher covering of wasting humanity.

Its a new addage to some of you, but it will ever hold true, "that the whitest person or thing on earth is the ones that has purity of the soul."

That a special races condition should be presented under the title of "The White Negro," is the farther object of this book, and under the idea that white is the true significance of purity I present you for further consideration " The White Negro," as will be discussed under the following heads in ten chapters:

I—The White Negro.

II—Is barbarous Africa the original home of the Negro?

III—Are the intellectual faculties of the Negro essentially inferior to those of the White?

IV—Will the Negro become amalgamated with, the White?

V—Demagogue's sentiment.

VI—Negro justice in blood.

VII—A Freeman, and yet a slave.

VIII—Position of the Press and Pulpit toward the Negro.

IX—Progress of the Negro.

X—An honest plea for the Negro.

Barbarous Africa not the Original Home of the Negro; but he is the descendant of Civilization and Intelligence.

II.

EGYPT is a country which is remarkable by characteristics entirely peculiar; rich in the wonders of nature and art, and the mother county of knowledge and civilization in the western world.

The population and civilization of Egypt are almost as ancient as the Deluge. When Abraham journeyed to this land, he found there already a well regulated state and a luxurious court. Lower Egypt, which is younger in its existence than the valley of the Nile, was thickly populated, which could only come about by the works of centuries, the mass of this population being the descendants of Ham, as Herodotus' description of their corporeal structure proves, corresponds with that of the Negro.

That the sons and daughters of Africa were barbarians from the beginning of time, is a mistake. They were not such, or all history is false in what it records of the human race. Speculation as to the correctness of the biblical version of the confusion of tongues and the separation of races, in the earliest ages of which we have any published account, would be in vain. That the Negro race inhabited the continent of Africa is a question beyond dispute, but that they have always been ignorant, barbarous and brutal is not sustained by any competent authority extant.

Whatever may have been the blood of Cleopatra, whose arts led captive Mark Antony and defied the authority of the Caesars, it cannot be questioned that she followed in the foot-steps of the ancient Africa princess of Egypt. Although the black races of Northern Africa were driven across the desert and despoiled of their possessions, so did the power of the White race decline in Southern Europe; and the whole world was involved in darkness for many generations.

The Negro lost his power in Egypt from civil strife, fomented and encouraged by the grasping avarice of foreign powers; and yet, through this defeat, in their retreat they carried with them a knowledge of mechanical arts and processes, which have gradually been lost as the cloud of ignorance and superstition settled over the people. They built cities the ruins of which are yet to be found; they had great and elaborate works of art, and were successful as agriculturists. There are yet to be found evidences of ancient religious training, showing that the races sprang from a parentage which believed in a Supreme Being.

But as contact with the world was forgotten, barbarism became the role; and in the place of an abode of learning and useful arts, the " Dark Continent" has supplied the world with the most lamentable examples of human misery and the most hideous instances of crime. As a strong community preyed upon a weak, and men and women were constantly made captives in war, even the savage heart became sated with rapine and butchery, and their reduction of captives to a condition of slavery followed just as naturally as the darkness of night follows the light of day.

Civilization has reigned in barbarous Africa, though it is silenced to-day, for in the fourteenth century, when Vasco de Gama made a voyage resulting in the discovery of Natal, Mozambique and a number of small islands on the coast of Africa, he found a people who enjoyed a high state of commercial advancement, and very many of the evidences of civilization which had come to them from the reign of Cleopatra and the time wherein the Caesars ruled Egypt. With their banishment they had not degenerated into a savage state, but had maintained a fair degree of the eminent civilization which pervaded Northern Africa in the palmy days of the splendor and refinement of their forefathers.

With the discoveries made by different nations and especially those of the British, there has been no fact brought to light which will gainsay the theory that the Negro races of Africa, however barbarized or unlettered, have been participants in civilized condition of society at some distant era.

Those tribes which have been most oppressed, and made the subjects of incursions by more powerful hands in the interests of slave traders, have sunk deepest in degradation. Those that have been able to maintain a well regulated system of defense, and to keep at bay predatory incursionists, present to the strangers who have visited them the evidences of natural superiority and the unmistakable indications of having known a better day.

It would be manifestly unjust to the Negro people of America for this discussion of what Africa has been in the past to be closed without calling attention to a criticism which has been often indulged, even by men holding high places in the Government. The objection has been raised against the Negro (*as a distinctive feature of the human race*), that his subjugation and reduction to a condition of slavery constituted an unanswerable argument against his capacity for maintaing a high standard of excellence after having arrived at such an eminence.

Surely this view has not been well taken, and facts certainly will not support it; because Africa has been the seat of learning, and has been peopled by a race who builded cities and towns, and monuments of greatness, and after the lapse of ages her population became dispersed, her knowledge of learning destroyed and the genius of her great inventors brought to naught, it cannot be said that other people of various races have not suffered the same degeneration and humiliation.

The researches which have been made upon American soil teach the unmistakable lesson that in this land there once existed a nation, or nations, very highly cultured. The buried cities which have been brought to light tell the story of lost greatness in terms that cannot be misunderstood, which the researches of the past and present will clearly show when investigated.

Therefore, this line of thought and deduction has been pursued by the writer with a view of convincing doubtful minds who may take time to peruse this little volume that the Negro is capable of the highest degree of civilization, and that the dusky people of African abstraction can maintain a place with honor alongside of the most famous nations of the globe, as they have done.

All that is required to prove the force and truth of such a theory is to give the Negro a fair opportunity in life with those men that reign in power.

Are the Intellectual Faculties of the Negro Essentially Inferior to those of the Whites?

III.

MAY I ask, are the intellectual faculties of the different nations inhabiting the globe, inferior to those of the Caucasian, who in a great many instances have claimed their superiority? It is a question of great doubt in the minds of many, and, in short, it is a very consoling fact to know that this state of unequal capacities now attributed to the several classes of mankind was not originally their first state.

If there is an all-wise and just God, who called into existence the universe and replenished it according to His desires, and in placing man thereon would endow him with different degrees of intellect to be distributed in each succeeding generation, making some competent to accomplish all things that they may be disposed to apply their hands to, and with this predestined power enabling them to take advantage of their fellow-men, making such the slaves or vices of this specially favored race, making their brother opponents, literally speaking, idiots, and the contestants of already superior race; I say if this could be true, the atonement instituted by the Savior, and intended for all mankind alike, has most assuredly come short of its intention, and the doctrine of predestination on the part of God could from this theory be established. So, even in accordance with Divine Providence, we observe that this theory is of little established rank.

That the Anglo-Saxon race have always been civilized, and the most progressive race on the globe, and this is to be determined by their present superiority, is a statement wanting of careful consideration. All nations, to a greater or less extent, have emerged from the wanton exiles of barbarism; even the Saxon himself is not an exception to this rule. For just at the beginning of the third century we find them emerging into existence of civilization, and reforming from their worship of images and Paganism to the true religion, Christianity.

I hope we may not affirm from this brief history of the Anglo-Saxons that this was their first existence, though it is the last from which they have grown to their present state to-day. Nor must we conclude that the Negro had no previous existence, but originated and continues in growth from barbarous Africa, leaning as a support and guide on the intellectual faculties of his Caucasian brother, for this is a wide mistake. Surely this is not so, for just before the reign of Caesars began at Rome, the seat of civilization and learning was in upper Africa. There philosophy was taught, temples were built, monuments were raised and wonders performed which have excited the admiration of the world during subsequent times.

Who built the pyramids? What knowledge of mechanics did they possess by means of which solid stones of the dimensions of forty thousand, nine hundred and sixty cubic feet, weighing four million, five hundred and eighty thousand, five hundred and twenty pounds, or nearly two thousand three hundred tons, were elevated one hundred feet above the earth and placed in a solid wall? Great men did this thing, and if we may believe the instruction of clearly convincing circumstances, these men were Negroes.

The Afro-American of the present day is quite like his Anglo-American brother, for in the veins of the Negro is running blood which has flown for centuries, though uncultivated, through the veins of some of the greatest thinkers of the earth, though his intellectual faculties have been somewhat confused from want of cultivation coming down through the mutation of centuries.

All those who may be acquainted with the Negro are familiar with his oppressed and exiled state of the past, and are aware of the fact that he requires cultivation of his intellectual faculties, which, I am glad to say, is in progress, and is being improved by him every day of his existence. Education and cultivation have made the advancement and progress of all nations who have ever reached their zenith.

This is the true key to Egyptian, Grecian and Roman monumental learning, and must be of nations to come; this has been the example and method pursued for centuries by the Anglos, and so far as meted out to the Negroes, considering the untold difficulties of the past, he is compared to-day almost on an equality with his Caucasian brother.

It is an absurdity to the intelligence of enlightened people, to accept the prejudiced theories presented in these ways against the race, before they have fully given the condemned the just opportunity to redeem that which he is rightly inherited to, but of which he has been deprived.

The great scientists, Melle and Barth, in their discoveries have made us sufficiently acquainted with this subject to prove that the most strongly characterized Negro, the typical Negro, has the power of raising himself to a considerable advanced condition, though it has been said by others that, without being a savage, he has remained a barbarian, as was the case with our German or Gallish ancestors. This view is not at all a just one, for the Negro has risen much higher. The annals of Amed Baba* show that in the Middle Ages the basin of the Niger contained empires very little inferior, in many respects, to European kingdoms of the same epoch.

And yet, has not the Negro, during his twenty-five years of freedom, climbed the ladder of fame side by side with, and made the same advancement as his Caucasian brother? Shall the great deeds recorded of the brilliant lives of such men as Crispus Attucks Frederic Douglass, Toussaint L'Overture and others of equal standing, be ignored ? Nay, never, for the lives of such men are pure, brave, noble, and worthy of the highest praise, never to be forgotten in the annels of their race, which should follow in their foot-prints.

You may cite your Tennyson, Webster or Clay, but remember that each is the standard of only one in the history of this great world; such men have never been repeated, even in the fairer race itself. But the Negro, with the same opportunity and his natural genius, is bound not only to be recognized as an intellectual equal, but superiority he is sure to gain.

---

*__*Editor's Note:*__ The "Amed Baba" referenced is likely Ahmed Baba al-Timbukti who lived in the 16th and early 17th century at the "basin of the Niger" which is Timbuktu, Mali. He was an indigenous Sub-Saharan African man of great intellect of the Sanhaja Berber ethnic group, and this contradicts the Eurocentric view of the savage, unintelligent African. The Sanhaja Berber ethnic group were conquered and converted to Islam during the Arab conquests in 7th and 8th centuries, far earlier before Ahmed Baba's life. It was at the University of Sankore which was located in Timbuktu, Mali where Ahmed Baba was chancellor and an author of several* *manuscripts before the University of Sankore was destroyed by the invading Moroccan Songhai people.*

Will the Negro Race become Amalgamated with the White Race!

IV.

IT IS with timidity, and from an unbiased position, that the author takes up this subject, which has been shunned, apparently, by so many writers.

First, let us accept as an established fact that all the different classes of mankind inhabiting the earth are the descendants of one parentage, having the power to cross and intermix; therefore being of the same species. This course of intermixture has been in progress ever since the beginning of time, and seems to be one of the traits of nature; in fact, has not this been the custom of all ancient nations, especially in the case of the Israelites while in the land of Canaan, as well as Rome, Greece and Pompeii? Wherever the different classes or races have been permitted to commingle, amalgamation of the weaker one into the superior has always been the result. For illustration let us take the different races of America to-day, and compare its present inhabitants with those of about two centuries ago, who were then, aside from the Indians, wholly of European descent. Do we find that to be the case at the present time? No, far different. Other nationalities have out grown these, and they have recrossed until it is impossible to find a descendant of the pure English blood of but one century ago.

And is not this also true in the case of the Negro? Though, as a whole, he has never in one instance that is recorded of him, attempted to mix his race with the Caucasian or any other. Yet we must submit and bear the blame. Let us go back to the time of the first landing of the Negro as a slave, bound in chains, and imported to this country; what were then his characteristics? Simply a coal black and burly Negro, the original species of his brother in Africa. Here he was placed in a pen by himself, absolutely surrounded by a white populace; to depend for his wants upon the mercy of his oppressors, and to suffer at their cruel hands. By force and by advantage taken of him by his Anglo-American brother, he was stolen from the home of his birth and joy, placed in a land of fair skins, in a heathenish and degrading state, and deprived of all his rights without his voice or consent. And in this self-damnable state, a curse before God and man, for over two centuries have seduction, rape and adultery, by force and without his consent, been practiced upon the Negro race in this civilized, enlightened and progressive America.

Hence, year by year, with this state of affairs, there has been bleached out a lighter and fairer octoroon American. Now such could not come about from the Black race alone. Then where do these mixed breeds all the way from Negro to the White originate? I leave this momentous question to be answered by my readers, drawing your conclusions from the preceding remarks.

In the year 1861, California*, observing this state of things, not only with the Negro, but with other races as well, became alarmed and passed a bill in their Legislature declaring that any white person convicted of having cohabited with or married a Negro, Chinese, or Indian had forfeited all his rights and become subject to all the Constitutional incapacities imposed upon men of color.* The local press announced very plainly that the object of this measure was the prevention of the fusion and amalgamation of the races.

Now, it is a fact that there are not over a dozen original Africans, if that many, in the United States to-day. Then what has become of about three hundred and thirty thousands of the Blacks who were imported to this country in the last two hundred years? If there are, according to statistics, over eight millions in the United States to-day, it well accounts for the contrast of color in comparison with their great growth.

Again let me present to your notice the fact that if three hundred and thirty thousand were originally brought to this country, and there are at the presen time over eight million Negroes here, two-thirds of these being of mixed blood, the progress of growth has been very rapid. This being the case, what will prevent them, in course of time, from complete amalgamation, especially as there is no more African immigration to this country?

The White race has enslaved the Negro and taken him with him to all parts of the globe, and where the local races have consented to intermix with the enslaved race, in every case they have produced races of the two-third species. In America the mulatto is born beside the octoroon, and in South America where Blacks, Whites and natives have long been in contact and have intermingled more freely, there are whole states in which half breeds are in the majority, and where it is extremely difficult to find a native of pure blood.

Have subterfuges or precautions been necessary to form these unions to insure the fertility and protection of the offspring? Quite the contrary. The tyranny of the Whites and the crimes of slavery afford sufficient proof that in this case fertility was not dependent upon circumstances, but simply upon the physical connection between all men, from the lowest of the Negroes to the first of the Whites. Mr. Hombron, the great scientist, says, from his observation during four years spent in Peru, Brazil and Chili, that unions of Whites with native American women have given the highest average of births, next come the Negro and Negress, and thirdly, the Negro and the native American woman. Unions between native Americans give the lowest average.

Hence, what is there to prevent, in course of time, the bleaching of our race into another, when the two are penned together, without the importation of any of the weaker race? Nothing whatever.

The Caucasian race have been the instigators of this as well as other monstrosities of which they have been guilty; and according to the provisions laid down by a free and democratic republic, and sustained by the Constitution, and as God, who knows all things, has created all men alike, in his own image, the conclusion is that any human being, be he Negro or Caucasian. Italian or German, Swede or Indian, whenever he has formed mixed breeds, this class forming a race by themselves, have the right, according to an honest judgement, to amalgamate with any race, regardless of color, state or position. This question is rapidly approaching a crisis in the United States at the present time. So long as the Negro retains his colors, and is distinguished by it, there will always be strife between him and his Caucasian brother. Hence, the sooner the race becomes one, the sooner will the race problem be solved.

Editor's Note: *The California law of 1861 that the author is possibly referring to is the Nevada 1861 Territorial Act which covered that area of California as well. Section 3 of this law means to have any white person in cohabitation with any non-white person "forfeit all his rights as a white person, and shall, for all legal purposes, be treated as a person of* *color." Therefore, this type of interracial mixing was criminalized with the punishment being treated like a non-white, being oppressed and placed in a lower class in society for education, employment, and even rights anywhere in the area, including court.*

A DEMAGOGUE'S SENTIMENT.

V.

One of the most important articles which I have recently read, and which is worthy the careful consideration of not only the black man against whom it is written, but of every human soul possessing the first principles of benevolence, is as follows:

Atlanta Constitution, (Dem.) April 25, 1892, "The President's action in making himself ex officio chairman of a New York Negro committee engaged in the compilation of campaign material intended to array Northern public opinion against the South, is about the meanest thing that a Republican partisan has ever been guilty of, as the Chicago Times puts it."

"The Southern outrage factory has been stock: campaign material for the Republican party ever since the period of reconstruction, but never has there been so cool-blooded a proposition as that which the President makes to the Negroes. It is, in substance, that they shall become, without expense to him, the compilers of campaign material, which shall fire the Northern heart at the proper time in the Presidential canvass. It is a cool-blooded outrage perpetrated by a small politician to serve his purely selfish aims. The President of the American people" (the Negro, I sup¬ pose, is not included?) "deliberately promises a party of Negro politicians that when they furnish him with their one-sided story of alleged" (not actual) "Southern outrages upon their race, he will insist in creating public sentiment that will make such outrages impossible." (Would that be more than right?)

"There has never been anything like this in our history before." (That is, since the days of the rebellion.) "When General Grant was President, he heard of an alleged outrage upon the Blacks in Louisiana. The Republican leaders raised a howl, and asked him what he was going to do about it." (Undoubtedly you mean by this that the Republicans are the Negroe's friends, and you, the Democrats, are his oppressor.) "He looked into the matter, and talked with some of his old soldiers, truthful, many fellows, and satisfied himself that the Whites were clearly justified. That was enough for him, and he refused to do anything. Moreover, he expressed his admiring approval of the pluck of the Louisianans, and said that they had done just exactly right." (Now, if he did sanction this unlawful act of mob law, my opinion is that his was a more perverted mind than the unblemished and spotless one of President Benjamin Harrison, whom you try to criticise and advise.)

"Gen'l Grant understood the situation, and he was very human, with no cold and flabby nonsence about him. A brave and true man, though a stalwart Republican, ought to be able to sympathize with his fellow countryman in the South, when they suffer such irreparable and horrible wrongs at the hands of the black brutes that they are almost nameless and cannot be narrated in print. The average Southerner is a good citizen," (I wonder where they got their ideal) "but when he returns to his plantation or village home, after a day's work, to find that his wife or little girl has fallen a victim to some prowling Negro outlaw, nothing but swift and terrible justice will satisfy him. His neighbors share his feeling, and make his cause their own."

"Human nature, Mr. President, cannot stand everything; the husbands, fathers and brothers of the South, sir, have the same affection for their loved ones that you and your Republican friends of the North feel toward the female members of your families. They are satisfied—they know—that you would do just what they do, if you were similarly situated; some crimes must be punished, or the result will be anarchy. The punishment must be swift and certain; the law's delay, the chances of defective indictments, escape from jail, the absence or death of an important witness, must not be risked."

"When the perpetrator of the foulest and most demonical of all crimes is captured and identified, we pity the mistaken judgment that would interfere with the noble private vengence which serves the public, serves virtue, and serves justice better than any other human agency could. Think this over, Mr. President, and embrace the first opportunity of saying to your Negro followers: ' When you cease to be midnight assassins and ravishers you will have no more outrages to complain of. If you are determined to maintain a secret crusade of murder against your white neighbors, your benefactors who give you work,'" (and thereby encourage the Southern white man's laziness) " and who are taxed for your education and support;" (forgetting that the Negro pays over one hundred and sixty-five million dollars taxes on his real estate, to say nothing of public schools and other public buildings,) "if you despoil their homes, then you will be left to your fate, and all races, all parties and all good men will applaud the terrible punishment visited upon you for your revolting crimes."

" When your heart prompts you to say that, you will, indeed, be a man, and a leader of men."

Quite graphically, indeed, is the Negro represented by his white assailants of the South, and if the people of this great commonwealth were ignorant of the true state of affairs in the Southern districts, such appeals might receive a place of sympathy in the heart or every law abiding citizen. It is not bad enough for such outrages as this vituperative scratcher speaks of to be committed without any interference, but these ideas must be forced upon the minds of every American citizen who has raised his right arm under the oath, for protection of equal rights to all men alike, as prescribed in the Constitution to protect, which the life blood of so many was spilt.

The inconsistent writer of the *Atlanta Constitution* has the audacity to quote the actions of Gen'l Grant, when he was President, by saying that when he heard of an alleged outrage upon the Blacks of Louisiana he gave the matter an investigation, and finding the Whites clearly justified, he refused to do anything; moreover he expressed his admiring approval of the pluck of the Louisianians, and said they had done exactly right. Other people remember the same occurences, and know it to be untrue.

How easy it is to write a few lies behind a dead man's back, for you that made this assertion well know that you had not the manhood to stand up before the valor of that grand old veteran, Ulysses S. Grant, and even breathe such assertions, much less quote them. Yet, suppose we admit this to be true, the Negro well remembers that this same Grant did give them protection in the outlawing South by establishing standing armies in their behalf.

I wonder what idea he is trying to convey when he is so egotistic as to say that the average Southerner is a good citizen. If a man openly rebels against the true principles of his government; if he will enslave his brother and treat him inhumanly; if he places no value upon human life; if he has the audacity to veto the support for the protectors and saviors of this united country, can you, in the broadest sense of the term, call such a man an average good citizen? At least, we know one thing, that this is only the Southerner's biased view of the ideal citizen.

Yes, it is a horrible thing for a white woman or little girl to be outraged by a Negro. But will such sympathizers as this writer seeks please reflect back to days of bondage and darkness, when the mothers and daughters of African extraction, helpless in the clutches 'of those unmerciful and brutal curs of the South, were robbed of their virtue? Follow me to our public schools, and I assure you that we will find Negroes there—at least so classed—from the various shades of black to shades so nearly white that the distinction is unobservable; pray, what may be the true cauese of all this?* It certainly could not have come about by the Negroes alone; and hence we can but force our ungodly masters to acknowledge their responsibility in the matter.

Now, when the same state of affairs is presented to you, you say: "Nothing but swift and terrible vengeance will satisfy you." Human nature, Mr. President, cannot stand everything. The husbands, fathers and brothers have the same affection for their loved ones that you and your republican friends of the North feel toward the female members of your families.

This is true, and I assure you all that the Negroes, as a whole, sympathize with you ; but can you not apply this same principle back about thirty years ago, when we were imposed upon in the same manner, and yet worse? How many mothers, daughters, fathers, sons and brothers were snatched from the hearts of their beloved, and sold into regions unknown? And many of these poor souls have never met or been united around their family hearths since.

Now, if your human nature cannot stand so much, and some crimes must be unlawfully punished; if this must be swift and certain, as the law's delay, the chances of defective indictments, escapes from jail, and the absence or death of an important witness must not be risked ; and as you pity the mistaken judgment that would interfere with the noble private vengeance which serves the public, serves virtue and serves justice better than any other human agency could, I can only prophesy, in accordance with the statements made by the veteran father of our race, Hon. Frederic Douglass, that a few more years of this continued oppression which human nature cannot endure, will result in turning out Negro anarchists and bomb throwers, which will be another annoyance for your weak and frail natures to endure. Your exhortation to the President may be warrantable; I have no refutation to offer; neither do I offer any apology for these wrongs committed by the Negroes; whose tendencies have been justly inherited, for every Negro believes in the law of heredity; but the sooner the Chief Executive acts in regard to the race problem, especially in the South, the better.

And as one identified with this brutal race, I expect ever to stand for their rights, and, if necessary, die for them, as thousands of others are willing, yea, anxious to lay down their lives for the same cause. And although the would-be-Senator of Colorado, named Teller, says in regard to the Lodge Bill, that a more infamous bill never passed the thresholds of the Senate,, he must not forget that some one—even himself, if he were able to do so— may be glad to pass a bill more just and radical than the infamous Force Bill,—so called—before another National Congress.

Editor's Note: When the author speaks on Negroes being various shades of black to shades so nearly white that it's indistinguishable from actual white people, this was and still is a very overlooked reality in the United States whenever people speak on the lineage of Black Americans versus the race of Black Americans. In many countries around the globe, a white looking person would be considered white because of the outer appearance. However, with Black Americans, who are also known as African Americans, Ethnic Black Americans, Afro Americans, Black and also Foundational Black Americans – all of which are endonyms for this specific ethnic group – they aren't solely defined by race. They are known by ethnic lineage which allows for the skin to look white in appearance and still be what was known back then as Negro. This is due to the one-drop rule to which no other ethnic group in the world fell under except the lineage of Black Americans. There were even enslaved who appeared white but were Ethnic Black American due to the womb law of that time for enslaved women.

NEGRO JUSTICE IN BLOOD.

VI.

IF THE majority must rule, is there any justice for the minority in the United States? This, of course depends largely from the scource in which the latter is found. Every honest American will admit that there is a partisan strife between the two original inhabitants of this country, which has existed ever since the days of slavery, and the Negro was granted freedom, not equal rights, and it now appears to the minds of many that such strife the government has encouraged by its laxness to act on either side.

The Constitution declares that all men are born equal, endowed with certain inalienable rights. Hence, this is the standard by which all men alike should submit, but do not, because there has never been an effort put forth to demand the same. Therefore, if this be a wrong standard under which man must submit without justice, it is high time that this government should ratify the same in such a manner as to give equal protection to her subjects according to what the majority say, and not for the sympathies, feelings or fears of the minority.

In giving the Negro his freedom he was not given an existence so long as he is disempowered with the voice to protect that freedom. This he does not receive and the fault lies not on his part, for where he is largely in the majority* and should have an active voice, here it is that his greatest oppression in the form of lawlessness, outrages and many other crimes come; wherein if he was once given that which this government has promised him, freedom he then would have. I now in plain emphasis speak of the South. Oh, but, says one, such a reform is too soon, and never will be accepted by the people of the South. Bosh! Both of these theories, as well as many others presented, to my mind are quite erroneous. Must a wrong of any kind be upheld, because biased hearted and prejudiced people will not see the truth, and obey the laws made by the majority under which they live? Was not the defeat of the late rebellion sufficient to impress their wrongs, with also the advancement of the Nineteenth Century announcing the same with all the firmness as did the colonists of the revolution in 1776?* The constitution says freedom and protection for all her subjects. Now if this they do not obtain, the fault yet lies with a cowardly government for failing to demand by force, if no other way, that which it has recorded in black and white upon her statutes. Pray do not make such writings a curse to American institutions. How easy it is to stir the pity of every human heart to realize the condition of the starving Russians, and many other human sympathies abroad, of which I condemn none, but for the many outrages committed in your doors of a more horrible character, you fail to raise your voice in the proper way for to check them. Within four years over 2,000 Negroes have been lynched and riddled with the contents of Winchester rifles, and not a word on the part of the government for the violation of her statutes or sorrow for these deeds has ever been expressed. Quite a wholesale murder indeed, and all American subjects, too, living under the protection of the red, white and blue, and which I fear has more meaning than merely the color designates. Here are three cases in particular of recent date, and within three months in which I wish to present to the minds of those

Americans who say they believe in justice, a freedom loving people, and whose hearts appear to be so overflown with sympathies that they have to express them universally abroad. In Omaha, Neb., but two months ago, a burly Negro, so stated, who was accused of committing rape on a girl, was taken from a county jail and hung dead, to a lamp post in the prominent part of the city. Again, but a few weeks later, another burly Negro fell a victim to an outrageous mob in Arkansas, so charged with only attempting to commit adultery on a white woman. This Negro's fate is quite different from any other on record, for, after strangling him with a rope, he was fettered hand and foot to a stump, saturated with petroleum, and then this statute of modesty and refinement, the victim of his outrage, steps forward from that hellish crowd, and, striking the flames from a parlor match, attaches it to two parts of that human being, though he may have been as guilty as any wretch. In the face of this I can only ask, where has the modesty of womankind gone? for she appears to be advancing beyond the limits of Jesse James, and I can- but pray that the deeds of that wretched female will haunt her to the brink of the grave.

On the 8th of March the telegraph reported the death of three more burly Negros. Dragged from the county jail of Memphis, Tenn , and through the streets of that cursed city until the limbs were severed from their bodies and eyeballs wrenched from their sockets, they were hanged, and then receiving their usual dose of Winchester exterminator, wrere left completely mutilated.

Now here are several facts of importance to be taken in consideration, first, that the attempt by the burly Negro (as he is called and is becoming quite a chestnut) to commit rape; he never accomplished it, but only attempts, yet for this must meet an unlawful death. Then, again, when one stops to give these attempts common sense judgment, it is not very queer that this monstrous beast of a burly Negro never accomplishes his deed; though his victim is but a delicate and weakly woman all alone with this large beast, all of which he is made by the press and others. Hence after all, this may account for why the mob law is meted out to him, rather than give him the justice of the civil Courts; for remember there are two sides to all questions, be they ever so wrong.

Again when men who are vested writh the power and responsibility to execute the laws of the government, become so currupt and mean as to lead these mob bands, while others give their consent by non interference, I think it is about time that the wronged, themselves, shall call a halt to such actions. Now I do not attempt to say, that every Negro that has unjustly met his death, was not guilty of the crime for which he was charged; but, I do say, that if this government is to be ruled by a system of laws, and these laws are vested that in the hands of men chosen to execute them, law should be permitted to meet its cause, or else' do away with the same, and every man being put under the law for his own protection, may then die bravely under his own efforts for defense and the protection of his alwise creator.

Hence so long as you keep the inferior in some respects coward down by fear of an unjust law, and permit others to interpret and execute this law to suit themselves, I can justly say, is the reason that so little trouble so far from the Negro has been experienced. May I then ask why it is that the people of the United States expect the Negro to be so loyal, submissive and obedient to the laws which the Caucasian makes, and cannot live up to himself, after the principles of law and government are bred into the very marrow of their bones for centuries?

While the Negro from over 250 years of oppression, ignorance and barbarism, thus released, must be more subserviant to these laws than the white man who makes them, and this I think that all cannot help but admit. Now is there any justice in this? I say no, for out of the 8,000,000 Negroes if one violates any law of a criminal character death is the immediate result. But for the 53,000,000 white population, with thousands committing the same crimes every day, yet for him there is some of their kind of justice. Though the Negro has always been true to his own master and now to the government, do you think he is always going to remain so when those who should give him justice are his greatest oppressors? No, and the crisis of the past and present depredations are close at hand, for the Negro has already concluded that the end, whatever it may be, can be no worse than his present condition.

In fact, without a proper head to a government, as well as all other institutions, with the welfare for the good of all his subjects at heart, the Negro may never expect either justice or protection from that source.

It has not been in the past except in but two instances, our grand emancipator and statesman, Abraham Lincoln, and General Grant. In the present case this is clearly seen by the non-expression of the President of the United States in regard to the wrongs imposed upon the Negro. Now, my brethren, as the national campaign is very near at hand, I can safely say that these evils may be partially remied by electing a chief executive of this nation who has the welfare of our race at heart. This issue is of more importance to us than, any other in the platforms. Then let us keep our eyes on the man that advocates tnis principle and be sure that he is the star to lead us, not out of Egypt, but from the present oppressions and wrongs inflicted upon us to-day, not only in the sunny South, but in the rugged North as well.

***Editor's Note:** When the author states "where he is largely in the majority", he is directing the readers' attention to the locations in the Southern United States of America where Black Americans (Negroes) were actually the majority, outnumbering whites at the time – such as South Carolina and Mississippi and prior to 1894, Louisiana. He could also be including the region called the Black Belt where Black Americans were highly concentrated in specific areas from Virginia to the Deep South.*

***Editor's Note:** "The colonists of the revolution in 1776" only wanted direct representation from those who were elected from their own specific communities, which aligns with the no taxation without representation phrase. If the British were to have governed the colonists from afar, then the colonists were aware that they would be governed by a majority and treated unfairly as a minority due to the British not understanding and taking into serious consideration their colonist needs. The author compares this same ideology to Black American citizens being able to have representation (electing their own from their own communities) and freedom along the same lines as the colonists did for their own people.*

A FREEMAN, AND YET A SLAVE.

VII.

WHAT DO I mean by liberty and freedom? Let me explain. If a men is prevented from going where he desires by a high mountain or rushing river or wild beasts, he is not enslaved; but if a man stands on the opposite shore of a stream and says that the other shall not cross, that is slavery. And this is the exact position of the Negro in America to-day. It is true that by law, or rather, by the Constitution, he has been set free from the outward form of bondage, and is said to have the equal freedom of all liberated men.

The former may be true, but I doubt the latter. Freedom, in reality, means more than a name or some writing; an assembly may draw up any kind of a document to grant certain privileges, but without the proper power and enforcement of the same, will justice or the liberty to exercise the prerogatives granted be enforced by the oppressor in favor of the one who is deprived of this freedom? No, quite the contrary. For instance, you have delivered the Negro from his bondage in slavery, investing him with the rights of all men in a free and protective republic; yet this government does not protect him in exercising the liberty of this so-called freedom. To substantiate the above assertion, within twenty-seven years over three thousand Negro lives have been unlawfully taken, and the publicly known assassins, under covering of law abiding citizens, have never been called into question or punished for such crimes by the Government, when the means lay in their power, and the voices of eight millions of the surviving wronged have constantly petitioned to the benevolent hearts of that government for protection, but have thus far failed in all their efforts to obtain it.

Follow me to the rugged South, and what do we find? As soon as the Mason and Dixon line has been crossed, the black man, regardless of his rightful position, standing or influence, is forced to humble himself to the lowest depths possible for a human creature. If on a journey, he is forced by the laws of this free government to take a smoking saloon, or some other apartment arranged for him, leaving the comfortable coach in which he may have traveled for miles, paying the same as any other passenger; his wife or daughters, be they ever so refined, must also make abode with low white men of all grades and habits, and if it be a hundred miles they have to journey, it alters not the case with them, they must put up with this indecency or not go at all.

Follow me a little further, and what will you see? Going to a tavern or hotel for a repast, be the Negro's looks and dress ever so respectable and clean, he is forced to eat in the kitchen, take his lunch in his hands and go out doors to eat it, or some other way equally as bad or worse. But please remember that he is obliged to pay the same for his accommodations as his white brother, be he what he may, who will be escorted to a handsome dining hall, with the ample accommodations of finely finished parlors, and comfortable rooms in which to retire. For sleeping accommodations, the Negro must repose in the streets*, or per chance find a friend of his own color in the community, or be taken up for a vagabond, compelled to pay a fine, or perhaps, worked out such fine in jail.

If he seeks conveyance to some distant part of the city, the street car or cab is hailed; if a white man is with him the conveyance stops, but only the white man is admitted; the black man is left to resume his journey on foot. This act is publicly practiced every day in the states of Alabama and Kentucky, by laws entered upon the statute books of those states by the minority, not the majority, consent of the people.

No wonder that the white rascals of that district do not wish to give the Negro power where he is in the majority, for if their own course of actions were once forced upon them probably they would learn to appreciate the rights which they steal from others.

If, while en route through the streets of the city, the Negro meets a white man he is obliged to step off the walk and give him the full course of action, and if acquainted must politely tip his hat. If he refuses to do so he is insulted, and if he resents such treatment he is arrested, fined and sent to jail, and if his resentment can be construed as a criminal offense he is or fettered and bound out on some plantation to suffer the cruel treatment of a cowardly overseer, which is the same as slavery, and in many instances worse, for the time of this confinement is much longer than a just law and an honest judge would permit for such a crime.

Election day arrives, and if he attempts to vote in accordance with the party of his choice, if the same be opposed by the majority of his oppressors, (as it always is), he is either shot at the polls as the result of a riot, sought by an armed posse in the lonely hours of the night, strung up by the neck and riddled with the contents of Winchester rifles.

The cry from many is that these things all happen in the South; but the writer thinks this quite a false statement. Let us examine their condition in the North; is the appearance of things changed any? Only in a very few respects. How many hotels, restaurants, and other resorts open to the public, will give him accommodation? Go to the Capital city itself, and you will find such places very scarce and far between. Having seen these things, you ask breathlessly: "How can this be? Have not the fourteenth and fifteenth amendments pronounced equal rights and protection to all mankind alike, regardless of race, color or past conditions?"

Oh, yes, the Constitution has so pronounced it, it is true, but its provisions have been in only a very few instances enforced. Hence, under the consideration of the same, and according to the fourteenth and fifteenth amendments, which state as follows: " No state shall deprive any person of life, liberty or property, without due process of law, nor deny any person in its jurisdiction the equal protection of the laws," if no state according to the federal statutes, has the right to deny protection to any person in any jurisdiction, why is it that during the year of 1880, one hundred and eighteen Negroes met their death by foul means, without the interference of the governors of the states where these outrages were committed, and in the year 1892, up to the present writing, one hundred and twenty-three more of these unfortunate Negros have publicly met their death by mob violence? Yet when the colored delegates from New York City went to Washington to memoralize the President regarding the outrages in the South, the President said in reply, " that the Federal Government could not interfere with the jurisdiction of state courts in the punishment of crimes committed within the limits of a state, and for that reason he had no power to act."

Then, does not this anul the fourteenth amendment previously stated? Can any reasonable, thinking person see any justice in such a law giving any state the right to murder two hundred and sixty of her subjects within twenty-four months, and allowing no interference on the part of the Federal Government?

Will you now attempt to refute my argument that the Negro is "A Freeman, and yet a Slave;" by presenting this last plea against it, that in the days of slavery Negroes were sold, but now they are not? Pray, what may be the meaning of this?

Fayette, Mo., March 28.

"A sale under the vagrant act* took place in Fayette this afternoon, when three Negroes were sold on the block to the highest bidder. One brought twenty-five dollars, another five dollars, and the third one dollar. The Negro element is highly indignant, and threaten to have revenge on the " po white trash," as they term them. The city officials have resolved to do away with the lazy Negroes."

This is a fair statement of the situation in the solid South, where the native white born element are all lazy, but none of them are sold on the block. This is the spirit that established slavery, and ought to be a sufficient warning to all Negroes as to the present feeling toward them. As I have previously stated, the Negro has a certain degree of freedom, but not the liberty to enjoy it. It is true that the southern states were made to retreat from certain measures about twenty-seven years ago, but I believe they are not conquered sufficiently yet, for they hold the power, and use it in car[r]ying out any measure they may so please to do.

This government makes so much noise over a few lives lost in a foreign country, or over the lives of a few seals, but has she ever as a whole, called into question the three thousand and more lives of her own subjects who have suffered unlawful deaths? Quite the contrary, though I suppose because it was done by their own hands it is all right. The German, Irish, Swede, or any other nationality except the Negro and Chinaman, may have all the rights the United States afford; but why these exceptions ? On the part of the Negro, it is his color and past condition only, which is now becoming to mean, " My once inferiors are my equals, and will, if given the proper or equal opportunities, be my superiors." Cross the waters to where our European brothers live, and this feeling is just the reverse; every man is recognized by his influence, position or financial circumstances.

Hence, there is but one principle of true freedom, which is this:

"True freedom is to share,
All the chains our brothers wear;
And with heart and hand to be
Anxious to make others free."

***Editor's Note:** The Negro Motorist Green Book was published in 1936, decades after the incidents noted in this quote by the author: "For sleeping accommodations, the Negro must repose in the streets". Traveling was dire at this time (1800s) for Black Americans due to Jim Crow/Black Code laws and segregation. If Black Americans didn't have a place to rest their heads while on the road traveling, they would have to make their beds outside. This motivated the publication of The Negro Motorist Green Book by Victor Hugo Green which mapped out safest routes for Black travelers in the USA.*

***Editor's Note:** "The Vagrant Act" mentioned by the author where "Negroes were sold on the block to the highest bidder" happened after emancipation. These vagrancy laws were mostly state held and fell under what is known as the oppressive Black Codes targeting Black Americans who didn't have a job. If they didn't have work, the vagrancy laws made that a crime, thus free Black Americans were arrested, made criminal and placed into slavery.*

Position of the Press and Pulpit towards the Colored Americans.

VIII.

To THOSE living since the issue of the Emancipation Proclamation, or whose experience has been closely associated with the public's sentiment since the year sixty-three, such persons will be more able to sympathize with the subjects of this chapter than some others, as it is further developed.

This subject now under consideration shall be discussed under two divisions, viz: "The Press," and "The Pulpit."

Ever since civilization has been known among men, there has always been some prime motor which has wielded the greater portion of public sentiment. In times when writing had not received its birth, signs and words were forcibly used to bring about the same results as the writing of this present day.

In this latter age—at about the dawning of the twentieth century, that period which shall supercede all other ages of the past in her developments—men are blessed with the invention of printing; and with cultivated minds that are imported from the colleges of our land every year, filled with sciences, history, and wit, and freshened with a spirit of eagerness as they launch out into the fields of life, they are over riding the multitudes of the ignorant until the station of honor and influence by them has been gained. And with the uniting of these two—brain and the art of printing—they are a mighty power in moulding public sentiments as well as human destinies.

Without the press the general world would be in ignorance, as one-half would not know what the other half was doing, and every happening would be a new experience to each community; while as things are now arranged, the thoughts of one people may be readily communicated to another within the limits of twenty-four hours.

The Press has also been the agitator as well as the benefactor of some of the most important questions of the land, a few of which are independance, war, tariff, temperance, slavery, and equal rights. The three latter ones being the most repulsive to public acceptation, innumerable means and plans have been exhausted on both sides of these questions, and still the agitation continues.

Societies have been organized, and their doctrines have been exponded to a generous public in the most forcible manner, and still the object for which they most earnestly seek has not as yet been attained; yet during this great struggle for right the press, the noiseless but powerful spokesman of the world has been constantly at work presenting its phase of the question regardless of its right or wrong.

And this is the greatest difficulty with the press that I can find, for like all other human agencies it is not infallible, and like many other societies who have been striving to help the cause money has been their greatest temptation, self honor their highest ambition, and injustice for those whom they have pretended to help is their all.

If there really could be found men of but one principle possessed with benevolent hearts and philanthropic spirits, and these could be induced to take hold of the workings of the press, then, might all men glory in the cause which they should espouse, for justice to all, and malice for none would be given regardless of circumstances, color, state or condition.

The question now is, what position has the press taken towards the colored people of America? But before we can fully answer this question, it will be necessary for us to understand its classification, and we find that the press may be classified under three divisions, viz: Political, which is its self divided into two branches, viz : Republican and Democratic. The other main branch of press work is that known as Religious, and taking their sentiments as a whole, we find they remain now as they always have in the past, one third for, and two thirds opposed to the colored races prosperity. Now this has come about from different causes, part of which may well be attributed to prejudice, popularity and personal gain. These three may, authoratively be called the main root of it all, for it is a well demonstrated fact that men will stoop to do most anything, be it ever so low or mean, in order that they may gain that one thing honor, which has been the mortifyer of many, and obtain that other idol of this world, money, which has been the destruction of many.

Thus the press of this country being arrayed on either side of this question, one as the Democratic, Cecessionists, or anti-equal rights men; the other Republican, Protectionists and equal rights men*, have in but a few exceptions done all they possibly could for the dethronement of the colored race in the affections of the American people.

Vituperation and abuse are constantly hurled at them, and in times when they are oppressed, when lawless hangmen by the thousands run loose throughout the land, making the colored people the prey of their vengence; yes, when tortures, barbarians, and heathen are permitted to take human creatures, often innocent ones, and repeatedly cremate them alive, without mercy and without law, surpassing by far the inquisition cruelties, and the dark chamber practices of ancient days, and the Press that powerful and influetial organ of public sentiment remains mum and silent; in the face of all this, I can but say that the press is not doing justice to the down trodden colored people of America, and in the spirit of the hopeful my fellow comrades remember that if this source to which we have to look for help fail us, there is yet hope. For the good and gracious God who rules, and created us for some future purpose is still holding us in reserve for the accomplishment of that end. And with all these obstacles before us let us again be consoled in the language of the poet:

"That God moves in a mysterous way

His wonders to perform,
He plants his foot-steps in the sea,
And rides upon the storms."

The proof of these truthful sayings have been so forcibly illustrated in the past, that I would dare but say, it is impossible for any one to deny the validity of the same.

From the gloom of bondage to the birth of freedom, from the threshold of freedom to almost the plains of equality have we come. Hence the thought may arise from this perplexing situation, and ask: What is it that is performing this silent development? We turn to observe our earthy benefactors, and find that the leven of progression comes not from this source; but again recalling those sublime thoughts of the poet:

" God moves in a mysterious way
His wonders to perform,
He plants his foot-steps in the sea.
And rides upon the storms."

We cannot help but attribute this all to God, and if he has performed such wonders for us in the past, with patient and determined hope let me say, he will do much more for us in the near future. Thus we find the press numerically could help and should help the colored race out of their present difficulties; but yet they have not and apparently will not help us.

Hence, go on unsympathizing editors
With the senseless quill in your hands;
Cry down, or leave undone by silence
That at which human hearts do rend.
And in the end if your conscience

Now fails to make amends,
Just remember that the righteous
Bar of God cannot help but heap
Coals of eternal burning
Upon your wearied heads.
—(Original by Author.)

We now direct our attention to the second division of this chapter which shall be devoted to the pulpit and its attitude towards the Colored American. And here I am compelled to pause once more, for the proper consideration of this subject before pronouncing my condemnation or commendation.

You have carefully followed my course of logic in the discussion of the press, and you have now stored away in your minds the gist of it all, and while I feel the full scope of the power that can be wielded by the press, I too can more fully realize the power of the pulpit when wielded in behalf of the down trodden and fallen children of God.

To me there is all the difference in the world between the press and the pulpit, for their basis of operation are built upon different grounds. The one is of a human call, the other a Godly call. The one a bias mission, the other the Nazarene mission.

With the press self says: Go ye therefor into all nations baptizing them in your wit for money and honor, but with the pulpit God says: "Go ye therefore and teach all nations, baptizing them in the name of the Father, and of the Son, and of the Holy Ghost." And again the bible says: " God has made of one blood all nations that dwell upon the face of the earth," also, "Go ye into all the world, and preach the gospel to every creature." From these passages of Scripture we may understand that beyond conscience the press as moral teachers have not that devine command to fulfill which the pulpit has, and while we can in many instances excuse the press for their neglect of duty, yet for the pulpit there is no neutral grounds, as is taught by the bible, and hence there should be none encouraged by men.

I know there will be many excuses presented by those who do not perform the will of God, but to whom the above words may apply, and some will say, our commission is to preach for the salvation of souls, and not the abuses of the age.

This may be the understanding of some clergymen who misinterpret the bible, like many of those who lived during the dark days of barbarous slavery, and taught the poor ignorant slaves, " that servants should obey their (earthly) masters,'1 and although they teach such doctrine of a simular nature at this late day, one cannot help but say that they are only heaping coals of damnation on their own souls. For there are few theologians of this century that would encourage such spurious doctrines, and when men are blessed with all facilities for enlightment upon the book of God, and do not apply themselves to it, such men or ministers are base demons, hypocrites, and false teachers, preaching only those doctrines which pleases the ears of those to whom they are called, and is instilling those false ideas into those who are more ignorant than themselves, that they may be practiced out upon the humble and helpless colored man.

Is it possible that if St. Paul, Peter or John the Baptist should come back to this world and behold the practices of men that they would direct their attention towards tariff, science, society, liquor, and many other things of the same nature denouncing the evil practices of these, when day after day, and week after week, month after month, and year after year, there are thousands of the most inhuman and unchristlike depredations performed on humanity that a world full of religion has ever known, and in the face of all this, men of this century who claim they are called of God to preach his word, to extoll the words of balm, and comfort to the distressed, wretched and wicked, will from one Lord's day to the dawn of another select their texts from the bible, and if there is some great political happening that has stirred the world with enthusiasm, they will apply this text to the same and preach such sermons two times a day.

Some of these orations, which they may be properly called, are of such a popular nature that on the Monday following, every leading news paper of any note in the land will be spreading these elaborate thoughts of some Divine known as a D. D., B. D., A. M., or L. L. D., throughout the whole world.

While on the other hand, if a human being of color be hung to a lamp post, shot down in prison, or repeatedly be burnt at the stake by mobs, and it matters not how cruel or immoral the act may be, I have for the first time yet to read or hear one of our leading devines denounce in the language of the gospel such ungodly practices. Those who even make the attempt to speak of these things handle them so timidly and fearfully with kid gloves, that two hours after the words have fallen from their lips their effect is no more than the chaff cast to the winds.

Again I say, would the apostle Paul be found so cowardly and inactive? No, for with more fire and power of the Holy Ghost, and eloquence that of old, would he, as he sat in the seat of the acropolis denouncing the Athenians with their idolitrous worshiping, climb to the highest pinicle of this world and in the most eloquent language proclaim a risen Savior, and denounce the evil practices of this demon world.

Thus in like manner it should be with the Christian pulpits of the present day. God has sent his servants into the world to better and elevate it, instead of encouraging and identifying themselves with it.

Our ministry well know the fact that the mode in which the churches are conducted to-day is not the example of Christ's model when he assembled together both Jew and Gentile, and worshiped with them together; but how different is this with our christian churches. For instance, how many white churches* to-day will extend the hospitality and especially the fellowship of their services to the colored races, and from a heart of welcome show to them by their actions that this is God's house, souls are the objects of our labors, and all who will may come and drink of the water of life freely.

Oh I fear! that there is not one to be found in the United States, and when I say this, I well realize the fact that I have said a big mouth full; but experience has proven this to me as well as the many testimonials of others, and it would only be necessary for me at this writing to go to the city of Mt. Pleasant, Iowa, a distance of only one hundred and seventy miles, and there I could produce you an example of a colored man who wished to identify himself with the First M. E. Church of that city, and on the account of color the minister as well as the majority of his flock refused to extend him their right hand of fellowship, and thus this precious soul was excluded from the house of God. Nor is this the only instance of a similar nature, for we do not find this alone in the Negro hating south, as the example of which I am now speaking are all happenings of the free North. It was during a large revival held in one of our leading cities that a poor, old, colored woman was observed to be under the influence of conviction in the rear part of the chapel where the meetings were carried on, and the news of this soul's condition was shortly communicated to the minister who with the advice of the officers of the church requested that a special bench be reserved in one part of the house separate from the other mourners for this helpless soul who had fallen under conviction of the higher powers. The idea of men making the mourner's bench a place of racial distinctions for the indwelling of the Holy Ghost.

Will you then tell me that the encouragement of such by the pulpit is right, or Christlike, when their conscience if no more tell them otherwise? I say no, no, no, and all who are guilty of such charges are like those spoken of in the bible: "Their judgment is going on before hand."

Nearly everyone is acquainted with the division of the M. E. Church North, and the M. E. Church South. This division was not the outgrowth of some biblical theme, but simply the acceptation of the slavery platform, and so sated in these abominable practices of human slavery were the Southern clergy, that they withdrew their filial relations from their brothers of the same creeds in the North.

Going back farther than this, we find in the history of this same church, that they excluded by force the colored people from their services, even in the silent hours of prayer were they dejected, and from these actions have sprung that church which has grown among the colored people somewhat like the stone hewn from the mountain without hands, and is now known as the A. M. E's. with a thousand four hundred and thirty-two of her own ministry, and two hundred and sixty-six thousand, four hundred and nineteen communicants.

Now if the above facts be true then the Christian Religion of the present day is carried out on sectarian basis, and instead of our love being supreme towards God, and our neighbors as ourselves; it is for the classes either of color, or wealth, and no such persons according to the bible can see God, nor even taste the wasting winds that may protrude from the portals of heaven. For how can we ever love or receive into our eternal fellowship in heaven those persons whom our earthly affections always disdained here on earth. Did not God send Philip in the spirit of the Holy Ghost to the eunuch of Persia to preach to him the risen Savior as well as his other apostles to the Jews and Gentiles? Yes it is a truth, and he has sent the Caucasian to preach and help the poor fallen weaklings of Ham your brother, that "as Christ was lifted up," so may they also be drawn up to him. For the bible makes prominent the father-hood of God, and the brother-hood of man. All middle walls of partition are broken down, all distinctions of class, condition, sex, color or nationonality are obliterated; whether Jew or Greek, Barbarian Seythian, all are one in Christ. The gospel adapted to all, is to be preached to all, prayers are offered for all, and the whole church are taught to pray for the coming of God's kingdom, and that his will may be done on earth as it is done in heaven. And if God's will is to be obeyed on earth by his ministers, then they will unite themselves regardless of color or sect, and put forth those efforts both in word and action for the abolishing of the evil practices of men and the consumation of Christ's kingdom. By them alone can the greatest influence be wielded for the ameliorating of the prejudices, and wrongs heaped up on the colored people. Of course we cannot expect any great result to be obtained by the adoption of this principle by one or two pulpits of the land, for if their actions were not favorably received by the people, I am well aware of the fact that it would only end in the impeachment of that minister, and the derision of every newspaper in the land.

But in order to the success of such a project, let there be called a general convention of the ministers in America, and all resolve to adopt the same method for the crushing of racial oppression, and I'll assure you it will then be a successful accomplishment, and in the end all men of all nations, with the angels of glory before the white throne of righteousness will proclaim: " Glory to God in the highest, peace on earth, and good will to men."

***Editor's Note:** When the author states "the Democratic, Cecessionists, or anti-equal rights men; the other Republican, Protectionists and equal rights men", it points to how the political atmosphere was in the 1800s. It was at this time that Republicans **claimed** more for equal rights and Democrats **claimed** more for anti-equal rights. This changed coming into the 1900s as the New Deal supporting working class Americans and Civil Rights began to take front stage as well as Black Americans, starting in the late 1800s, started becoming unsettled with the obvious fact that the Republican party had already abandoned them – **only wanting their votes while giving them no power in politics**.*

Thus, Black Americans, in large numbers, moved to the Democratic Party in the 1900s which had shifted its stance to pro-equality while the white Southerners who felt abandoned fled the Democratic Party in revolt, to instead align with the Republican Party which shifted to the party of anti-equal and pro-white in the 1900s. This shift has remained through 2026 and will possibly remain this way for years to come due to the Republican Party of 2026 having nearly all white representation in Congress while the Democratic Party of 2026 is multiracial and multiethnic in Congress.

*The author, at the time of writing this book (1894), accused them **both** of harming Black Americans for their own gain. In the past, both parties had utilized their **press and power** to undermine Black Americans for gain and self-honor, remaining silent to the atrocities of that time period toward Black Americans, such as lynchings.*

***Editor's Note:** The author mentions "White churches" and questions how many would extend hospitality to colored races? At the time of his writing this book, not many white churches would extend any hospitality. This is why there was a creation of the White Church and Black Church in the United States of America. It was because white churches' Christianity failed at the point of the racial lines. Thus, Black Americans were forced to create their own places of worship, although and unlike white churches, they didn't ban white people from attending. White people simply didn't attend due to racism which is a form a sadism which goes against true Christianity, or being a disciple of Jesus Christ.*

For example, the A.M.E (African Methodist Episcopal) Church is the Black congregation and the M.E.(Methodist Episocopal) congregation is white.

PROGRESS OF THE NEGRO.

IX.

LIKE all other races the Negro is still in the line of progress. Not at the foot nor at the middle, but so closely to the top round of the ladder of advancement, that he may well be considered one of the first in rank.

The Negro like all other races has had his ups and downs; yet, in many respects his case presents a different aspect to the world than that of his now present competitors. For, to my mind there has never been a race of people who have made the same unlimited progress, under the same conditions, and in the same length of time, as the burly and hated Negro. Even his worst enemies will not attempt to deny this fact. And now, stretching before us under the great canopy of advancement; in legislative halls, in our school houses, at the mechanic's bench, in the field of produce, behind the plow, Yea! in every conceivable glen of industry, your vision can not but help behold not the crisis of the Negroe's progress; but only the faint beginning.

The question now may be asked, why is it that I commend one race and not another? Is this because of a special point of gain I wish to reap? Or is it because of the prejudice stirred up in me? My reply, dear friends, is neither. It is only from a heart enthralled with the gratitude of justice. It is from a motive pure and true as the qualities of tried gold. I might pause, it is true, and flatter the Caucasian, who would claim naturally to be first in the line of progress. Or, perhaps exalt the Mongolian to heights which he has never attained. Yet through the omniscient eye of the Almighty my wrong acts would be found out; while beneath the loathing of a guilty conscience, as an outcast I would feel condemned. So, as the Romans of old I will say, "Let justice to whom justice is due be given, for Caesar and his edicts must be obeyed.

Hence, once more taking up the narative, from which I have somewhat deviated, I am forced to a great pause, when I contemplate the Negroe's past or beginning. For here lies a germ planted, whose future was considered by the tillers only as an instrument to be used in the hands of others ; but if only those producers were living at this present day, they would now behold this worthless germ, so supposed, yielding the largest crop of any other seed in the world, and according to their number have superseded all classes in progress regardless of its size, color or principles.

Yes, from the exiles of barbarism have they come, out of the most ignorant haunts and darkest jungles of Africa by myriads were they brought, without sympathy, friends or money. By innumerable hosts did they continue to pour in upon our shores, until this fair America, the home of the brave, and the land of the free, was glouting in the brutish practice of human slavery, that which has stained her bright name and laid low the higher virtues, which could only crown her to be the pier in freedom of all nations.

Yet, while a biased minded people were still reveling in that atmosphere of God given freedom, (for which they through many sacrifices waded) did in the face of all this enslave and deprive of others that which they had just gained. But through all this, the just God who sees and rules all things still kept his omniscient eye upon the wicked doings of man, and inasmuch as they meted it out to others now should the same be meted out to them. For "Independence" among the colonists could now be heard as the cry rising up from all sources, and " that taxation without representation was tyranny."

In the midst of all this providence brought forth Crispus Attucks, a Negro slave, to challenge even Great Britan herself for the cause of Independence, and for this principle of right he bravely met his death as the first martyr of Independence, (not his own) but that of his Anglo-Saxon brothers, who, because he was endowed with the more supreme powers held his brother as a slave with the Revolutionists as conquerors in the great struggle, and not without the Negroe's aid either.

Again, was the Negro forged in chains of slavery, more debasing and cruel than had ever been known in the annals of civilized history neither before nor since, I would also have you to know that during the two hundred years or more in which the Negro was enslaved, he was not standing still, nor returning back to his misfortunate traits of the past; but instead was rapidly taking those strides, which were destined to make him a great and stable future. In the place of barbarism he partook the elements of civilization, and with this he adapted himself to the surrounding situations in proportion to the bounds allowed him.

On, On, did the conflict go, the Negro making higher strides of progress, until the question in all its fullness presented itself to an abased world; enquiring in the language of justice. Can there be both master and slave existing with individuals of the same right, durating under the same material and spiritual laws? This question was a monster, a weight of conscientious conviction on the one side, and a load too large for digestion on the other. Providence was now rapidly, but silently opening the way to which the Negro though ignorant was developing. God himself with mighty host had set in operation those instruments which would soon burst forth the clouds of gospel truth. The church and its ministry were the first causes put in action, and a mighty one she was too, with her martyrs of christlike zeal, and her saints of devotion, did she pour forth her denunciation of human servitude that " None shall be called master save God," and with the more powerful agencies of prayer the strong holds of mammon slavery were soon seen to shake, the press too began to cry aloud and when her ballasts were all turned loose, with full force the fortress of slavery was again seen to quake.

From every pulpit and rostrum the voices of Garrison, Wendell Phillips, Summer, and others could be heard thundering in words of logic their abhorence of the most diabolical criminal practices by men of intelligence that the world has ever known, and so powerful were their appeals that the whole world was stirred to the greatest depths of sympathy for the oppressed. The crisis had come. Legislative enactments had been propounded and enforced, the legions could lay under it no longer, secession was declared, Fort Sumpter had been fired, and a Jeff. Davis had been crowned, and the devil with all his host now perched himself on high defying God and his host of conquerors.

But where was Alexander before Egypt fell? Where was Cromwell before Charles I, died, and his position to rule was attained? Where was Napoleon before France was subdued? They were being reserved until their time of needfulness should come, and thus it was with old America and the Secessionists. God was holding in reserve Abraham Lincoln, Sherman, Grant and Seward who should dawn on their field of duty, and force to subjection the rebellions' sons Davis and Lee with their children, and to liberate those bondsmen who had served their untimely end as inferiors, and not equals, that they might pursue the line of progress equal to that of their Anglo-Saxon brother.

Thus with the fall of Richmond, and principally the year sixty-three Africa and her children have been marching on, on, on, migrating to the different state without money, friends, or shelter, but with all prejudice conceivable heaped upon his shoulders, he has from that time to the present age striven to keep pace with all other races who have even had the advantage of him, and as I have said I will repeat again with all frankness, that through all his past the Negro stands to-day second to no other race in the strides of progress.

His Real Estate taxes has accumulated to the sum of $130,000,000. The facilities of schooling in their own number seventeen schools and academies. In the professions they have Doctors, Lawyers, Professors and many others of other trades which I do not mention, and who are second to no other throughout the wide world and of whom any race may well be proud.

They are editing over two hundred newspapers in the United States alone, and in politics he makes no less a prominent figure. Many of them hold some of the most prominent positions in the Government, and as to their religious progress, I am pleased to say they are no more in the rear in this respect than other races, they have their own churches with their thousands of communicants, and some of the most able Devines in the world. Our business men, and farmers, and mechanics are increasing every year in proportion as the opportunities present themselves, and in many other ways which I have not stated we find the Negros are taking a great interest.

Remember all this has been accomplished within the last twenty-seven years, and if you will pardon me for the presumption, I will say that in the next twenty seven years the world will be more greatly astonished at his achievements than they are now at this present census. Thus I hope at the expiration of that time, that all prejudice against the darker races of man will have been wiped out, and happy may they then be the equals of all men still making their progression on to God.

AN HONEST PLEA FOR THE NEGRO.

X.

THE NEGRO differs from the Anglo-Saxon in color only; he has been educated by his surroundings, out of barbarism into the highest type of enlightenment, having had twenty-seven years of freedom in which to develop his faculties and obtain a fair recognition of his natural ability. It is now time that he should be given an opportunity.

He is of sanguine temperament, and he naturally looks upon the bright side of everything; he believes that his future is bright, and is willing, yea, anxious, to work out his own destiny. His position in America to-day is far from being a desirable one; if the Caucasian were regarded as an inferior by a ruling race, his instinct of liberty and his pride cultivated by a taste of freedom, would resist. The Negro after years of slavery, has all the more deeply inculcated into his temperament that love of freedom and that spirit of liberty of which Americans are so proud; he was once a bondsman, but now he is free. A reflection on the fact that if events had not transpired as they have, he would today, instead of breathing freedom's air, wear shackles of slavery, imbues him with that love of liberty. His ability would have no peer had he the years of cultivation and development of the white man.

Raised from the depths of barbarism*, he is capable, in one century, of standing in the Congressional halls of the mightiest nations of the earth, capable of representing his country in foreign fields of diplomacy, of writing deep and interesting articles for our great magazines, and of filling the loftiest pulpits of the land.

He has no desire to associate with his white neighbor further than for his own development; it is not social equality he is seeking, it is a chance to develop, caused by a desire to push forward. When he asks for a berth in a Pullman sleeper or a stateroom in one of the great steamers, it is not from a desire to associate with the white people, but because he wants comfort, because he believes he is worthy of it.

When he asks for a position as bank cashier or railroad conductor, it is because of an aspiration to rise to heights as yet-unattained; when he asks for a matriculation card at a college or university, it is not because he wants to become a social equal of whites, but because he has a desire for moral and intellectual cultivation.

He is beginning to realize that to subject himself to the rule of others is not the highest ideal of liberty; he has no desire to make laws for others, but to help to make them for himself, though here his wants are constantly ignored.

The plea of the white race, that of the inferior ability of the Negro in his intellectual and social respects, is one that deserves very little consideration, and it should be obnoxious to the intelligence of civilized people. What other race on the globe, who have grown from ignorance and superstition, without friends, money or homes to shelter them from the storms of this world, have, in twenty-five years, succeeded in gaining partial control of the reins which for centuries were used to lead them by?

What inducements has the Caucasian ever offered the Negro, to make him more than he is? Has he not availed himself of everything within his grasp? Yea; and much more; by education, which is the root of cultivation and civilization, he has risen from the more humble positions in life to be the Representatives of both the race and nation on the highest plains of diplomacy. Yet this plea goes on.

The real question is, have the white race done their duty? What better mission could be wished than this? How can the followers of such martyrs as Attucks, Abraham Lincoln, John Brown, and others whose cause and intentions were honest and true to the last, be so ignominiously ignored now?

Have you, with all the advancement of the nineteenth century, forgotten the dear records of the past and of the silent dead? Most assuredly it must be so; if not what has become of the measures involved in the Declaration of Independence? I pray you, do not, if you have not already, place yourselves upon the side from which came the oppression which you once resented. Give the Negro a fair show, and your plea will soon be answered.

To the people of the South, whose numbers are equaled by the Negroes, this colored population of law abiding citizens is especially obnoxious; what is the cause of this? Simply the fact that their once inferiors have risen to be their political and social equals, and that they are, as a class, from the nature of their makeup, energetic, industrious, and willing at all times to make their homes happy, comfortable and pleasant, as they were taught to make those of their masters, and as the ones that he sees grouping around him every day. Can you, from an honest heart, condemn him?

It is also true, and this fact being so important, must not be overlooked, that the Negroes as a whole, must depend upon daily labor for their livelihood, hence they yet have all the odds to contend with. Why do you not open to our intelligence your offices, and allow us positions which we are fully able to fill? You will not do so; you will even draw back with disgust, yet you are unable to tell why.

With this condition of affairs we find that the Southern white man hates the Negro, and the Northern Negro has no love for the white man. What, but trouble can be the result of all this? Being constantly urged on in his animosity and rancor by political fanatics of the North, who are actuated by a desire to further party interests at any cost, this condition of things will undoubtedly sooner or later come to crisis, and now is the time to prevent the great calamity. If, this question is such a barrier on both sides, the one fearing equal justice and supremacy, and the other fearing unjustness and inequality, there must be concessions from both sides, which I think should be on equal conditions.

Little did the colonists think that their oppression would be settled by means of the Revolutionary War but that the minute men were equal to the demands of the hour.

This being true why do we not avoid the errors of the past and act before the dreadful climax is reached? This idea of evolution, will never come to any peaceful solution, and I am sure that a great many of my colleagues who advocate this theory will soon be convinced of their present error in advocating such a solution of the race problem, and will change their course of action, and will discover measures to solve this touching question in a peaceful but honest and reasonable manner. The Negro has been down, and probably is down now, but he will not stay so.

Oh! I fear the day, left to itself that shall determine this question will be one of cries, of terror and helplessness, a day in which the swarth knife and sword will sup¬ plant the cannon, and homes will be drenched in atoning blood; when liberty will be no more, then, and not till then, will this question, left to itself, come to an end.

The Negro is an American the same as those of English and German descent; God has sent him here to stay, and He has a work for him to do here; here will his destiny be wrought out. He is devoted to his country; he is intensely patriotic, for there were no braver men in the army of the Union than the one hundred and seventy-five thousand Negro soldiers, and we to-day feel grateful toward the nation, notwithstanding the long years of bitter and debasing slavery, a gratitude that has no place in the hearts of the immigrants who c6me to us from foreign shores.

The Negro will never be an anarchist; history affords no other example of a people who have endured such shameless and inexcusable wrongs manifesting such devotion and affection for the nation at whose hands they have endured these wrongs. The Negro will suffer neglect at the hands of his country, but I do not believe he will ever betray it or rise up against it. When I remember the Haymarket riot of Chicago, and think to what deeds oppression and ignorance, desperation and godlessness may yet drive the great hordes of wretched workmen who have been brought from Europe to America to revolution, I can not but feel that Providence is holding in reserve the Negro, once the slave, to be the redeemer of our country in the vast and sad crisis that I fear will be rendered inevitable by the stupid moral ignorance of our politians and the blind selfishness of the Church.

I have long believed in the hour of trial, which is to try America and her institutions, in which class shall be arrayed against class; when this time comes, the Negro will acquit himself as a man and as an American who is worthy of his citizenship, and brave the tide.

It is therefore, the part of sound political wisdom and the foresight of Christian statesmanship, to believe that the safety of American institutions depends in more senses than one, upon the destiny of the Negroes who are struggling to disenthrall themselves from ignorance and escape the vice and moral wretchedness of the slavery into which the Caucasians have placed them. If there should ever come a time when law and order shall have to measure their strength with anarchy and violence in burning cities and on trampled fields, the Negro race will be found, almost to a man, standing for law and order and for the defense of our civil and religious institutions.

Hence, by a study of our prosperous growth and abundant gains, does not our future appear brighter than it ever seemed to you before? Why should it not be as encouraging as that of any of our brother races?

Then let us be encouraged to press forward, for out of Ethiopia will arise some day a second Toussaint L'Overture, who will lead his loyal and patriotic brethren to be the saviors of their country.

***Editor's Note:** Barbarism when it is written by the author is not meant to say Black people were born that way, but rather saying that they were oppressed, stereotyped and made that way via cruelty and violence, imposed, not inherent. For example, being considered barbaric for not having the ability to speak English like an Anglo-Saxon because the Black enslaved was being forced to forget another language which he was well educated in and learn a foreign one in another land with new rules of engagement while in chains, oppressed.*

THE FUTURE OF THE NEGRO.

XI.

THE PRESENT situation of the Negro race to-day presents both a bright and dark side. It is most encouraging with regard to the race itself, when judging from the past, for within less than a querter of a century the Negro has made wonderful progress, and his present condition as contrasted with his past exhibits an astonishing evolution, mentally, morally, physically and financially; even his worst enemies will not attempt a denial of this fact.

The questions to be considered are, what has the Negro done, what is he doing, and what will he do or be?

What has the Negro done? Well, what is it he has not accomplished that lay within his grasp? From the exile of barbarism and oppression for over two hundred and fifty years he has been the object of imposition and vengence which has been meted out to him by his oppressors, and as a martyr, often sacrificing his life to obtain his rights, the prejudice against him being so powerful at times that it swarms in the air like a pestilence of flies, from the mouths and hearts of men; yet this he is living to overcome.

To the traveler who visits the South, here the condition of the Negro presents itself in a forcible manner, not only in the presence of the Negro, but in years of irksome toil for which this Government owes him, but for which no compensation was ever given, and for which he receives no thanks or credit.

This condition of affairs has been a great barrier for the Negro to confront, considering his past condition from which he has been set free. Yet with all this upon him he has never raised his voice against these wrongs, but still survives, striving through his zealous efforts to gain a better future.

Hence, the evidence of the following remarks will go to prove the Negroe's struggling condition, his ascendency over his once superiors who are now compelled to become his equals, and in many respects his inferiors, not because it is the Negroes desire, but because it is not in his power to prevent it.

Said a prominent Northern lawyer, a Republican, to me recently: " I confess that I am disappointed in the Negro; he has had twenty-five years of freedom now, and what has he done with them?" "Mr. C—," I replied: "Your own Northern Emerson has said that to reform a man you must begin with his grandmother. We are just now dealing with the grandmothers." "I see," said he thoughtfully. But continuing the same insinuation, he said that "we are lascivious," why should we not be when our marital rights were ignored and invaded for centuries? "He said that we steal," why should we not when we ourselves were stolen? He said that we lie,'" why should we not, when for two hundred and forty years our word was not taken under oath? "He said we shirk," why should we not when for generations our only incentive to industry was the lash of the overseer?

Do you believe in heredity, or is that another one of the many things monopolized by the white man? I am ready to admit that the Negro is not so white as he has been painted by some of his sentimental friends; often he is dilatory, wasteful, slovenly, given to petty pilfering, disposed to live from hand to mouth, and is capable of obliterating an obligation as easily as a school-boy wipes a sum from a slate with a sponge; but if you do not know white men of the same kind, your experience has been an exceptionally happy one.

This is only one side of the shield; now let us see the other. Were it not as old a story to you as it is to me, I could tell you by the hour of Negroes who stayed by their mistresses and the children during that terrible five years when their masters were away; of Negroes that charged side by side with their masters in a fight which was none of theirs; of Negroes who shared their masters' imprisonment; of Negroes, one at least, who voluntarily, and in the face of many inducements and much opposition, walked back from Pennsylvania and freedom to South Carolina and servitude, because of a promise to a dead master to go "back to Miss Mary," of another who has related to me how, that on the night before the fatal fight, he "kivered up de Cunnel as wa'm as de thinness of de blankets would allow." Is there a more pathetic sentence in all history?

Who shall measure the depths of the love, or the height of the manhood of that black man as he handled those threadbare blankets, worn to holes in places, and then, regardless of himself, "'kivered up de Cunnel as wa'm as de thinness of the blankets would allow?" One of the whitest pages in all history is that which records the loyalty of the black man to his master and his master's wife and little ones during that long struggle, one object of which was to keep that black man a slave.

One of the blackest pages in all history, and almost a blank, is that which fails to record the championship of the black man's cause by a single representative Southern politician.

It is worse than idle to contend for the rights and citizenship of a people who constitute about one seventh of the whole population, and who were, almost to a man born in this country, some of them of a native ancestry of seven generations; people who pay taxes on a hundred and sixty millions of dollars, and who own in their own right thirteen colleges and academies of a respectable grade; who number among their ranks thousands of educated professional men, whom the leading institutions of learning have been delighted to honor; who raise about all the rice and cane, three fifths of the cotton and a fair share of the corn, to say nothing of the melons, potatoes, peanuts, and other crops; who capably pursue every mechanical occupation, and who are as essential to the South's existence as legs are to a pedestrian or arms to a blacksmith.

On my last trip through the South, only a few weeks before the present writing, I was told everywhere that the "nigger" wouldn't work. " Then," said I, "you have the most phenomenal crop in the world; a crop that plants itself, plows itself, bales itself and totes itself to the market.

To say nothing of all other crops and all other vocations, the Negroes of the South have raised this year (?) more than one bale of cotton per head, valued at about forty dollars. A very idle population this? The fact is that the whites of the sunny South have the most valuable working people on the face of the earth; they are docile, fairly industrious, cheap, and above all peaceful. An old saying has it: "You'll never miss the water till the well runs dry." The people of the South may realize this yet. I hope not, however, but it may come true.

But suppose we admit that the colored people of the South are all that is alleged against them; the question still remains, shall they be serfs or citizens? The answer is that this is America, and that her serfdom has no place for the sole of its foot. I say this is true too, and I am forced to record this honest conviction in the form of a statement in favor of the Negro.

Of course we must admit that this is the universal faith of the white men, and they all admit it, only in different forms. Follow the thinking brain of our nation to the Senate Chamber, and what is the sentiment there in regard to our race? Regardless, my dear readers, of political parties, just observe for a moment the last bill in our favor entitled the Lodge Document*, which was so vehemently defeated. It is a disgrace not only to this so-called free America, but to be the transaction of mortal men. The defeat of that bill means more than human words can express, and only goes to strengthen the cowardly and uncalled-for assertion made by Judge Taney in his decision in the Dred Scott case, in the State of Ohio. "That a Negro has no rights which a white man is bound to respect." Is this true? Did you ever stop to interpret the meaning of this bold assertion? Well, it means simply this, that the time has never come when a white man will be forced or obliged to respect them.

These difficulties mentioned in the statements which I have just made have all been encountered by the Negro in the past, and have been partially overcome; hence, are here brought to view that the Nation may see and correct its wrong. Indeed, the past contains horrors enough of its own, without speaking of the present or future: but as the wrongs inflicted upon an innocent and helpless one are bound, according to the just laws of the all wise Creator, to return to the ones who inflict them, I say to those who have always been free, that some day they will be called upon to repent for these wrongs.

You ask me then, what have the Government and the people at large not done of that which has been in their power to do? As I have already stated in a previous chapter, they have robbed them of over two generations' strength, and life with all its bliss and righteousness; you have turned him loose from bondage friendless, homeless, penniless, this woeful world to roam; you have cremated, butchered and slaughtered our promising and hopeful youth, and with all the obstacles of invention you have blocked his way. The spirit of the Caucasian in some respects, takes the likeness of the Pharisee, who prayed in a high place and bosted of all the good things he had done, imagining that it was building honor and glory to his name, and adding to his temporal gain. I say their spirit, from all outward appearances, is to missionize and lend a helping hand to those unfortunates who have not been blessed as they have; please tell me then why they have failed to observe home, and those around them, and why their attention is directed miles and miles beyond?

Let me tell you that their ultimate destiny will also be in that lake of brimstone and crimson, far, far beyond the place called heaven. When they loosed the shackles from the bondsman and told the slave to go free, why did they not provide schools for the Negro that he might become educated, that he might have the opportunity to learn the duties of a civilized man under a free government, if no more?

In what the Negro has, in many respects done, aside from his natural genius, he has been obliged to pattern after the Caucasian; then can or should he be condemned for the wrongs which he commits? Has there ever been a race of people who have made such progress in the same length of time as the burly and hated Negro? Nay, not one.

This is but a brief outline of the Afro-American's past; and yet the half has never been told. You ask me, then, what is the Negro doing? Trying to do the same as his other oppressed brethren, trying to overthrow the prejudices of the past; making a man of himself by gaining an education at his own expense, cultivating his morals by accepting the blessed gospel of Jesus Christ, collecting around him a great amount of this world's goods, in finance and other forms, and feeling that his constitution, ambition and zeal are equal to those of his Caucasian brother in enabling him to press forward. In short, the Negro is tired of ignorance, and is sensitive about being called ignorant. He is tired of being called foggy and superstitious. For where the opportunity is offered, he is more scrupulous as to the regular attendance of his children at the public schools than are the whites in many instances, which shows that they are in the line of progress with the rest of mankind.

The intelligent Negro realizes his past disadvantages, and is ready to take hold of whatever he can be made to see will conduce to the progress of his people, At the present time the better class of colored people are looking for just what the Caucasian has and what every race needs, the elevation of his position as a people. The Negro is neither better nor worse, morally, than any other race; he obeys bad and good impulses, as do others; he is one of the greatest scholars as well as one of the poorest; he is one of the most industrious and thrifty, as well as one of the most indolent; the color of his skin and the texture of his hair have nothing to do with his qualifications.

In spite of the great progress made by the Negro, there are some white people who have not yet come to understand these facts, although they are being brought face to face with them. The Negro's intelligence is blindly ignored, as are his rights, save when it serves some selfish purpose or ulterior design to admit their existence, and if he were not possessed of a steadfastness of purpose worthy of a higher recognition and encouragement than he receives, he would give up the struggle as useless; for in the face of his unquestioned advance, it is a fact to be noted that never before has his presence as a factor in great political questions been so apprehensively looked upon, or so generally regarded by the South as a serious disturbing factor in critical complications threatening dire results.

We may well stop to ask, how is this? Judging between the two great extremes of the country, the North refers the question to the South, whose people answer that it is due to their fear of Negro supremacy.

Is there any basis for this fear? None at all. That which the South declares it will not have Negro supremacy, has no part in the Negroes plans for his future, nor is it desired by him; he simply seeks to exercise and enjoy, undeterred, the freedom and rights guaranteed him as citizen by the Constitution; he leaves all else to the future evolution of just public sentiment and to private choice. As for ruling over the whites, the idea has never entered the minds of intelligent, thinking Negroes.

The Negro's future has also been presented in the form of emigration, but to the writer it is a very impracticable and foolish notion; for here you are again confronted by untold difficulties and obstacles, even if it was possible. If you will go back with me to the proceedings of the fifty-first Congress, we will find that an attempt was made by Senator Morgan, of Alabama, to introduce a bill to this effect, and it was considered by the majority of the thinking men of the country as an utter impossibility. If the eight million Negroes of the United States would all peaceably consent to these terms, it was found to be a fact that vessels for their shipment could not be procured in our docks, that the cost would exceed that of any previous war, and the risks would be unlimited.

Colored citizens of the United States, Africa is not our home any more than America is the home of the Indian alone; Africa is a garden of treasures and riches, it is true, but it will never do the American Negro, as a whole, any good.

Did not the Puritans kill off and exterminate the Indians when they came to this continent? Hence, observe the condition of the latter at the present day.

If the white man thinks that the Negro should go back to Africa because he was brought from there, why does he not go back to Europe, where he originally came from ? For the Indians objected to his coming and to his residence here just the same, and upon as plausible grounds as the whites object to the presence of the Negroes of the present day.

We must remember that Africa does not belong to the United States, for colonies from different nations, have about settled the land on the coast. Discoverers, explorers and treasure seekers are searching for all that is to be found; the climate is a peculiar one to which to become acclimated, and these colonies, living under the flags of different nations, will not give up their claims and rights to settle an established wrong fomented by certain sects of the populace in the United States.

Again, we must remember the great loss to our individual selves in such an undertaking; our possessions must be gotten rid of which would incur large expenses to the government; for if it would act fairly, these would have to be rightly disposed of.

As to crossing the great Atlantic, have you ever thought of how many bodies to-day lie sleeping in watery graves, in the briny and unfathomable recesses of the mighty deep? It is indeed, a fearful thing to think of, for in such an attempt parents and children, brothers and sisters, husband and wives will be separated forever. Have we not, as a people, been separated enough? Yes, and may a just God forbid the success of these evil projects and thoughts which are permitted to control the human minds.

One great fault lies with our people as a class; we have never shown the principles of our manhood enough, for we allowed ourselves to be enslaved, which is forbidden by nature; and to-day, with the position and standing we hold, we trust our welfare too largely to the Caucasian, who will not in the majority of cases, do that which is absolutely just and due to all mankind. We, in many instances, try to defend ourselves from criticisms of our past by the plea of our ignorance; that may do, but how is it with the American Indian? "No," says the Indian, "I will starve and die brave rather than be the white man's slave, or be otherwisely imposed upon." The Indians may be heathens, as they are generally called, but nevertheless they are possessed of that kind of material which teaches them to uphold and protect their God-given rights.

My brethren of color, I appeal to you to think twice before taking this wrong step of emigration*, and that at the preaching of a few fanatics, your enemies, who are undoubtedly well sallaried for their meager services put forth. Remember that there are more than one Judas Ischariot in this world, and as one betrayed the blessed Saviour, be careful that one does not betray you.

As I have previously stated, I still maintain, your future is in America and not in Africa. We are just getting a footing in this grand old Republic, for which our fathers and mothers died the deaths of martyrs ; will you now, when staring prosperity in the face, give up that which rightly belongs to you, because it is a sacrifice to retain it? No! never, I hope.

In nearly every city of the Union in which the Negroes are located, you find them with homes or trying to procure them, you find them conducting business for themselves; you find among them doctors, lawyers, musicians and farmers second to none in the world, and last, but not least, they competently occupy some of the most prominent positions in the land, editing over two hundred newspapers in the United States alone, and holding governmental positions at home and abroad.

Remember, this has all come about within the last twenty-five years; before that time your state was one of ignorance and wretchedness, and now, because you are refused a great many rights here that belong to you, and which are guaranteed to you by the Constitution, if you emigrate, imagining that there rests your future, you will make a sad mistake.

Then let us make true men of ourselves, and by having closer organizations, union of effort and competent men selected as leaders, our race may reach the place of influence to which it is entitled, and may do much to put down these wrongs perpetrated against us.

One thing yet we are lacking; we need more education, less politicians and office-seekers, more farmers and mechanics. Then, with that power of natural genius endowed in our hearts by the Creator, with that human pathos, that native eloquence and our power of fancy and imagination, all these of which our Anglo American brother is not possessed, I do not hesitate to say that our possibilities in the future are as great as those of the white man. If it is still true that time's noblest offspring is to be the last, we must look to the descendants of Father Ham's sons in America, instead of those of Japheth, for the last great act of the human drama, for, says a passage of Scripture: " Let but the angels of Bethlehem brood over the children of the DARK CONTINENT, singing their songs of peace and good will to men; let the cross be uplifted to them; let the heralds of salvation go with their feet of beauty through the land, and the God who made of one blood all men to dwell on all the face of the earth."

He only knows what their ultimate zenith will be; at any rate, it does not belong to the descendants of a people in whose veins may be flowing the blood of men who at the opening of the Christian era were offering human sacrifices.

One good characteristic of the Negro is meekness, and one beauty in one of our Lord's sayings: " Blessed are the meek, for they shall inherit the earth." Many of you may not believe it, but the great inheriting races have been people whose progress has been with garments rolled in blood; and it may yet be that the greatest race of the earth will yet rise under the banner of the "Prince of Peace." To some it seems impossible, but it may be true.

Thus the blessed poet, Longfellow, though no prophet, spake these truths that he knew would come true, (as they did before he died, in his poem entitled) "The Slave Singing at Midnight."

"Loud he sang the Psalm of David,
 He, a negro and enslaved ;
      Sang of Israel's victory,
      Sang of Zion, bright and free.

In that hour, when night is calmest,
Sang he from the Hebrew Psalmist,
      In a voice so sweet and clear
      That I could not choose but hear.

Paul and Silas, in their prison,
Sang of Christ the Lord arisen;
      And an earthquake's arm of might.
      Broke the dungeon's gate at night.

But, alas! what holy angel
Brings the slave this glad evangel ?
      And what earthquake's arm of might
      Breaks his dungeon's gate at night?"

And alas! did the angel loose those prisoner's hands, and slavery was no more.

Thus, as the reform of slavery has come and passed, let me say, though myself no prophet, that the oppression of the Negro at the present day, like the condition of slavery, will soon ignite and burst; the oppression is at its crisis. We have been, once, unprotected chattel property; we have been disfranchised in a republican government of forty-four states, fourteen of which we have made by the sweat of our brows; but have been deprived of the right to enjoy the results of our labors, and last but not least, we are murdered today by wholesale slaughter.

What more, now, can we expect? What more can be done? All are ready to admit that we are human beings, and as such, let me say that our natures, no more than those of the Caucasian race, cannot endure everything, and will, if the past practices are kept up rise in revolt. I hope that this will not be necessary, but it may be so. There is but one thing for us, as a people to do, and that is to organize, not in words but in activity. This can be effected, and if every Judas Iscariot we find in the ranks will not hang himself, let us delegate men from our number to do it. By making examples of a few traitors like this, I think a proper organization may be properly effected. All races have these organization, from the Caucasian down to the Chinamen. It is a fact that in certain parts of the South they are effecting organizations for the extermination of the Negroes, as is shown by the following:

Editor's Note: *The author's mention of the Lodge Document, also called the Lodge Bill which was, was the failed bill that was meant to protect Black Americans' voting rights and secure elections during Reconstruction in the South. Because of its failure, more Black Americans chose to leave the Republican Party as their needs were being ignored for the needs of others.*

__Editor's Note:__ The emigration the author is probably referring to what was known as the Back- to-Africa movement which occurred during the late 1800s, specifically to Liberia, a country that was founded earlier in the 1800s in a deal made by the American Colonization Society (white men) to the chiefs over the land of what would be known as Liberia in Africa. The indigenous chiefs were paid handsomely for the land in exchange for free Black Americans to emigrate there.

At the founding of Liberia in the early 1800s, the plan was to move only the free Black Americans there and keep the enslaved Black Americans in the South. It was the thought of the American Colonization Society and other white men that if they relocated free Black Americans from the United States, the enslaved Black Americans would lose hope. In the end, most Black Americans didn't volunteer to leave America, and in 1863, the Emancipation Proclamation was announced, effectively freeing the enslaved in the Southern states.

CAN THIS BE TRUE?

An Organization said to be formed to exterminate the Negro.

Birmingham, Ala., July 2.

An organization has been formed here known as the "Knights of the White Shield." About 250 men have been initiated into the order. The constitution narates the troubles with the Negroes and proposes to form alliances for the preservation of white supremacy. Nothing will be done in violation of United States and State Laws, but steps are to be taken to spread the order and rid the country of the Negro race.* Some of the prominent men of the city are members of the order.—(*Times, Buffalo, N, Y.*)

Then why should we not prepare for this great conflict which is to confront us? It is true that all odds are against us; the Negro is so mingled with different bloods and dispositions that we can hardly blame his non-unity; we are thus in many respects, a drawback to ourselves, we find some wishing to be Spaniards, Creoles, Octoroons and Blue-veins*, and sometimes I thank God that so many Negroes are being lynched; for it is teaching this peculiarly mixed race some sense, and is not uniting these Blue-veins, as they are called, to the Caucasian people, but dust to dust with the mobers' rope around their necks pulled by white men's hands.

Then again, I sympathize with these Blue-veins, for the Negro race seems to be cursed, and their species is not one to seek after or to be proud of. He is, it is true, burly, as the papers picture him, black, flat-nosed, with big thick lips, coarse features, large feet, wooly hair, etc., surely these are not to be desired, when placed in contrast to the physical characteristics of the Caucasian.

I know not why this is placed upon us, except it is to fulfill the prophecy of Noah to his sons: "That the sons of Ham should dwell in the tents and be the servant of his brothers," or to be a siege of trials set before us, as was with the children of Israel. I believe in prayer, and think if all churches and our people all over the world would accept Christ and labor for him, he will protect and deliver us. Hence, there is but one course left for us to pursue and that is this, let it be remembered that whether we be white, black, brown, red or yellow, the one-eighth drop of Negro blood will spoil a hogshead of white, as the Hon. Fred Douglas has said, and the white man also calls and classes us in this sense as Negroes just the same, and hence as Negroes, let us all work and co-operate with one another for our own good and welfare. Let us establish places of business, patronize these, and keep out of politics at the present. Institute night schools and educate our fathers to read and write, who have been disfranchised for the lack of these qualifications, and hence in time they may have the power of speech by the free casting of their ballot, and thus teach the white man of this country that we can outscheme all his legislation against us, and that too in the positions which rightly belong to us. Then with a united body let our motto be, not " United we stand as divided we fall," but, United we stand and United we fall in faith, hope and love, and thus we will lay the butresses for our coming prosperity to build a noble and grand future.

***Editor's Note:** To the right is a newspaper clipping from The Philadelphia Inquirer of 1892 which documents the beginnings of what the author writes as "Knights of the White Shield" and their objective to maintain the supremacy of the Caucasian race.*

KNIGHTS OF THE WHITE SHIELD.

Organized to Maintain the Supremacy of the Caucasian Race.

Special to The Inquirer.

BIRMINGHAM, Ala., July 3.—An oath-bound organization called Knights of the White Shield has been organized in this part of the country. More than 200 men of this place are already enrolled.

The purposes of the order are set forth in these extracts from a document which the applicant for admission is obliged to sign:

"We pledge our sacred honor, our fortune and our lives in fealty to the supremacy and honor of our Caucasian blood and white man's rule in all matters of race preference and race prejudice. We will, without regard to the past, present or future political preference or affiliation, ever exert ourselves to our utmost ability (not in violation of the laws of our State and of the United States) in fostering and sustaining the supremacy of our race in all matters political or social."

"KNIGHTS OF THE WHITE SHIELD"

An Organization Formed to "Rid the South of Negroes."

BIRMINGHAM, Ala., July 2.—An organization has been formed here known as the "Knights of the White Shield." About 250 men have been initiated into the order. The constitution narrates the trouble with the negroes, and proposes to form alliances for the preservation of white supremacy. Nothing will be done in violation of United States and state laws, but steps are to taken to rid the country of the negro race. Some of prominent men of the city are members of the order.

While another newspaper clipping from the Buffalo Post, Saturday, July 2nd of 1892 (located above) calls the same organization as one to "Rid the South of Negroes".

*__*Editor's Note:__ When the author mentions __Blue-veins__, this was a very light skinned black person with a high percentage of white, or European, ancestry who considered him or herself in another class, a higher racial class. They were called Blue-veins because they were so light they one could see their veins, yet they weren't white but mixed. Many times, in order to pass the Blue-vein test, one would have to showcase their blue veins to be set apart. The author states that they were called this by Caucasians, and he is also glad they were lynched along with Black people so they will forever remember that they are Black, reminding them they they are not viewed as better than Black people to the racist, but seen as the same by them.*

*Colorism was at its highest point in the United States in that point in time, and to be white was seen as the beauty standard. The author expresses this in the next paragraph when he states the physical characteristics of the Negro in comparison to the Caucasian. The author speaks of how he also feels sorry for the **Blue-veins** due to the fact that they have to live in a society where having Negro features is not as beautiful as Caucasian features. He feels sorry for Blue-veins because he understands that it **seems** a curse to have Negro features. He did not say that it **is** a curse, but only that it seems that way in American society. This makes him pity Blue-veins because they seem trapped, trying to escape something they can never; trying to be something that, in American society at that time was considered more beautiful – the Caucasian.*

That train of thought isn't superior in Black America today, for most of Black American society have reclaimed their own beauty from the harms of white supremacy into "Black and Proud" and "Black is Beautiful" as well as "Black Excellence". It is the Black American that made the word black around the world one to be admired and celebrated, and Black Culture, which is Black American culture, the most emulated globally on every continent.

EDITOR'S AFTERWORD ON

REVEREND M. W. THORNTON & GEORGE WHITE LYNCHING

The life of the young Reverend Montrose William Thornton was one of incredible attention due to his unique ability to capture audiences when he spoke and the daring way in which he spoke the truth, or what many of that time considered, his own truth. Rev. M.W. Thornton became a highly controversial pastor and preacher of the First A. M. E. Church in the early 1900s and even before that, but the focus will remain on the early 1900s when there was a grave lynching of a Black American man named George White.

Lynchings of that time period were brutally frequent, and the young reverend read and saw much during his time on earth that infuriated him. It was during the year 1903 in the month of June that a Black man by the name of George White was hunted down and lynched after being accused of raping and murdering a white lady, Helen Bishop. George White's lynching was so brutal and unjust that several Black preachers spoke out directly and fiercely on the matter. One of those preachers was Reverend M.W. Thornton.

When Reverend M.W. Thornton spoke up after the mob lynching of George White, many people tried to accuse him of inciting a riot against white people and also accused him of being a bad man and preacher. However, he was doing the opposite or inciting a riot. He instead was advising Black Americans to defend themselves against the fiends he called white lynchmen.

WILMINGTON LYNCHING

Dr. W. D. Crum, Collector of Charleston, South Carolina Port Speaks in Chicago.

Rev. Montrose Thornton's Sensational Sermon

Rev. Thornton of Wilmington, Del., is an Iowa Product and at One Time Lived in Des Moines. Dr. Bartlett of the First Congregational Church, Chicago on Lynching Advises His People to Arm and Defend Themselves as Outlaw Tracy Did.

Source: The Bystander Fri Jul 3, 1903 Page 1 Des Moines Iowa Part 2

THE DETAILS OF CORONER'S INVESTIGATION.

Says a Wilmington, Del., special of last Wednesday:

"Resolved, That George White came to his death between the hours of ten p. m., on June 22, 1903, and four a. m., June 23, 1903, by being burned in a field adjoining the road leading to the Ferris Industrial School by a party or parties unknown to the jury."

This verdict was rendered by the Coroner's Jury to-night at the close of an inquest of an absurd character.

No effort was made to obtain the names of those who led the mob that battered down the doors of the workhouse on Monday night and took the cowering negro, George White, from his cell and led him to the stake where he was burned amid the yells of the populace. There was no serious attempt to punish anybody. The temper of the crowd has been at fever heat and the local officials are glad enough to allow the matter to drop despite the storm of adverse comment.

As a result of the verdict and the popular clamor Arthur Corwell, the only prisoner, was released on bail despite the fact that the warant against him charged murder. He was admitted to bail in the sum of $5000 and upon gaining freedom he found himself a popular hero and a leader of men. He was received with a great ovation and carried away by a yelling multitude.

If he had not been so opportunely released there would have been a jail delivery to prove the disapproval of the crowd.

The factual story of what happened with George White is as follows, according to the details of coroner's investigation taken from *The Jeffersonian, Saturday June 27 1903, page 2(left)*:

The victim George White "came to his death" by violent lynching where he was set aflame by a mob of white men between late night and early morning- the hours of 10pm on June 22, 1903 and 4a.m. on June 23, 1903 – in a field near Ferris Industrial School.

The mob beat down the door to where George White was located (in a warehouse jail), kidnapped him and tied him with his hands behind his back and also feet tied and set him on fire. As he burned to death, while he was still alive, one of the white mobsters, in another report, hammered his head causing his immediate death.

The Evening Journal, Wilmington, Del; Wednesday, June 24, 1903

After his death, the crowd cut up the body of a charred Mr. George White and sold pieces of his body as relics around the entire town for one dollar. The courts had to try and find pieces of his body just to make it whole.

Whether George White was guilty or innocent of the rape and murder of a white lady wasn't discovered in court. What took place was mob justice, and his lynching in Wilmington, Delaware was one of the most gruesome, making headlines all across the United States of America. No one was convicted. The man who ended up the only prisoner of the lynching, Arthur Corwell, was released and treated as a hero. Meanwhile, more Black Americans were attacked as they walked the streets minding their

MOB ATTACKS NEGROES.

Most of the negroes had kept out of the way, but whenever one passed on a trolley he was greeted with jeers and yells. The first one who attempted to walk through Market street after the temper of the mob had been aroused was James Gale. He received a thousand blows and seeing an opening starter to run.

Some one in the crowd jabbed a knife into him and he fell with a piteous howl. He was kicked until some of the men about him interfered to save his life. Policemen were called and led him to a drug store, where his wounds were dressed. As he was afraid to go home alone Police Captain Kane went with him.

business. A Black man by the name of James Gale was beaten and stabbed by the mob of white lynchmen. Some other people in the area managed to save his life as the police officers got him into a drugstore to bandage his wounds.

Reverend M. W. Thornton, many would imagine, was extremely upset by the lynchings. This was a man who had already previously been outspoken about lynchings, even inside this particular book "The White Negro".

SOLD PART OF BODY

Horrible Relics Being Hawked Around the City.

Portions of White's body are in almost every part of town. Early yesterday morning people began taking sections of the negro's anatomy. One man with a club knocked the teeth from the skull and another cut the toes and fingers off. People were going about the city selling the toes and fingers at $1 apiece, and strange to say they met with a ready sale.

In a Front street saloon yesterday one of the thigh bones was on exhibition and at a business house on the same thoroughfare was displayed another part of the charred body. A man in the Twelfth ward secured one of the big and little toes of the man, and the others are distributed in different sections of the city, the owners claiming they will preserve them in alcohol. One of the feet is said to be in the possession of one of the men at the Eagle's Carnival. The gruesomeness does not strike one from the mere telling of these facts. To meet a man on the street and have him draw from his pocket a part of the burned negro and show it with apparent pride, is disgusting beyond words.

Therefore, it isn't far-fetched that he would have something to say and not hold his tongue about the brutal murder of George White. This is exactly what he did.

Inside the newspaper clipping from *The Evening Journal, Wilmington, Del; Wednesday, June 24, 1903* titled **"Sold Part of Body",** the article explains how the body parts of George White were met with "ready sale", meaning white people enjoyed buying parts of his body. They had his thigh bones on exhibit at a business house, and some buyers preserved pieces of his charred body in alcohol. Some white people even carried around parts of George White's body in their pockets, showing it off "with pride".

It is obvious that when they young Reverend M. W. Thornton lived through this disgrace, he would be not only upset but would not hold his tongue for the defense of his people against the mobs of white men across the United States who enjoy the murder of Black people via lynchings.

Muscatine News-Tribune Wednesday July 1, 1903 Page 1 Headline (right)

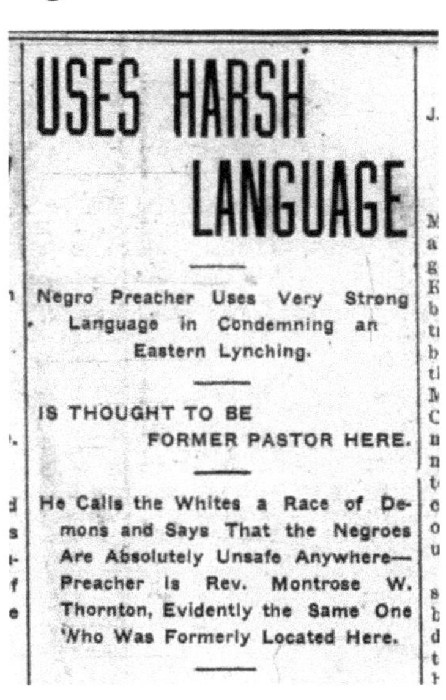

USES HARSH LANGUAGE

Negro Preacher Uses Very Strong Language in Condemning an Eastern Lynching.

IS THOUGHT TO BE FORMER PASTOR HERE.

He Calls the Whites a Race of Demons and Says That the Negroes Are Absolutely Unsafe Anywhere— Preacher Is Rev. Montrose W. Thornton, Evidently the Same One Who Was Formerly Located Here.

Therefore, he, in his rage, called for Black Americans to defend themselves because the United States will never do it. He is documented as calling white people a race a demons, and in context, he meant white people who perform these lynchings as a form of mob justice.

Reverend Thornton felt sincerely that there was no other option for Black Americans - whenever charged of a crime or even if they are innocent – to defend themselves.

[By Associated Press.]

Wilmington, Del., June 29.—White men were called demons and monsters by the Rev. M. W. Thornton, a colored preacher, here yesterday, in discussing the lynching of George White. The colored minister declared the only thing the negro could do to defend himself from mobs was to turn outlaw, and, like Tracy, die in his tracks, drinking the blood of his pursuers. The sermon was preached in the First African Methodist Episcopal church in this city, and it stirred the congregation to great excitement.

Mr. Thornton said: "The white man, in face of his boasted civilization, stands before my eyes tonight the demon of the world's races, a monster incarnate, and in so far as the negro race is concerned seems to give no quarter. The white is a heathen, a fiend, a monstrosity before God, and is equal to any act in the category of crime. I would sooner trust myself in a den of a hyena as in his arms.

"There is but one part left for the persecuted negro when charged with crime and when indecent. Be a law unto himself. You are taught by this lesson of courage to save yourselves from torture at the hands of the blood-seeking public. Save your race from insult and shame. Be your own sheriff, court and jury, as was the outlaw Tracy. Die in your tracks, perhaps drinking the blood of your pursuers. Booker T. Washington's charity, humanity, advice of forgiveness, love, industry and so on will never be reciprocated by white men."

When many at the time heard his words to be incendiary, if one understands the times and the weight that Black preachers had to carry in the midst of such violence, it seems that Reverend Thornton had come to his breaking point and may have even recalled the days of Ester in the Bible when God allowed Jews to defend themselves from the mob that had been waiting to wipe them from the face of the earth.

The Kalamazoo Gazette, Kalamazoo, Michigan, Tue, Jun 30, 1903 · Page 1 (above) reported the words of Rev. M. W. Thornton as he preached from the First African Methodist Episcopal church:

"The white man, in the face of his boasted civilization, stands before my eyes tonight the demon of the world's races, a monster incarnate, and in so far as the negro race is concerned

seems to give no quarter. The white is a heathen, a fiend, a monstrosity before God, and is equal to any act in the category of crime. I would sooner trust myself in the den of hyena than in his arms.

"There is but one part left for the persecuted negro when charged with crime and when indecent. Be a law unto himself. You are taught by this lesson of outrage to save yourselves from torture at the hands of the blood-seeking public. Save your race from insult and shame. Be your own sheriff, court and jury, as was the outlaw Tracy. Die in your tracks, perhaps drinking the blood of your pursuers. Booker T. Washington's charity, humanity, advice of forgiveness, love, industry and so on will never be reciprocated by white men."

Just by reading his sermon alone, many may have the thoughts that this man couldn't be the preacher that he proclaims to be, but upon inspection of what took place just days before and the sadistic lynching of George White, one can argue that his speech at the A.M.E. church was profound with grief, anger and weariness of having to tolerate such mob evil for far too long. A Black man was never sentenced to a fair trial - only execution for any crime. The written details are

THOUSANDS WITNESS BURNING AT STAKE OF GEORGE WHITE BY A MOB

County Workhouse Assaulted, Doors Battered Down and the Negro Secured in Spite of Determined Resistance---Is Dragged to the Scene of the Crime, Confessed to the Awful Deed and Had Purposed to Assault Another--Fire Built in the Field and the Negro Cried "God Help Me" as the Torch was Applied--Women-Witnessed the Burning. Cheers as He Perished.

preserved many newspapers, but none so detailed as *The Morning News, Wilmington, Delaware, June 23, 1903* (below) which headlined **"Thousands Witness Burning at Stake of George White by a Mob"**

Inside the subtitle of article, one can see that it was reported that George White had "confessed" to the murder of a white lady and even purposed to assault someone else, however, this isn't true. He was already seated in the warehouse jail awaiting a trial when terror beat in his door. Thousands of white men had him dragged him out of the jail after being allowed to enter by armed policemen who were supposed to be protecting White.

> Once inside the cell of the negro he was told that he had better confess, and he made a full and complete statement. Some of it was unfit to print, but the confession was complete. The negro said:

When the mob entered the cell, they *coerced a confession* from George White through terrorism.

> ROPE ABOUT HIS NECK.
> Having gotten the confession of the negro the mob tied a rope about his neck and one about his wrist and dragged him down stairs. He made a desperate fight and nearly overpowered seven men who were holding him. The crowd beat him and some of them were in favor of shooting but the leaders cried out.
> CRY TO BURN HIM.
> "Take him to the place and burn him," and followed by a crowd of perhaps eight thousand people the unfortunate negro was hauled to the place of execution. The road is dark and full of muddy holes but the negro was pulled over it as though he was so much wood.
> Along the road the negro made a desperate fight for his life but it was useless. Once or twice he nearly disabled

It was then that the mob placed a rope around Mr. George White's neck and hauled him out of the jailhouse with the intent on taking him to the scene of where the lady was murdered and setting him ablaze while still alive.

During this time, it is documented in the same newspaper that thousands were elated to see the Black man die by burning. Those who weren't close enough to see it shouted in irritation that they couldn't get a good look. There was a very sadistic desire in the mob of white people to watch a man who hadn't even gone to trial and had a forced confession burn at the stake.

The mob gave him one last chance to speak, and George White said a prayer, a prayer to which made many in the mob cry actually. It was then that White seemed to have given up and let what would happen occur.

He was burned to death right there before what was reported to be thousands of white people who clamored atop one another to see the sight of a Black man being burned alive in a field that couldn't even hold all of the crowd. It was a very sadistic scene as they feasted off of the murder of a man whom they forced confessions from, and later, the newspapers went on to report it as a confession although it was forced.

Many people were mortified in the Black American community because according to the law of the land, Mr. White should have had a fair trial, and not only that, the mob justice was a grave injustice as the main lynchmen all went free for the lynching.

Days Later, an Explanation of Reverend M.W. Thornton's Inflammatory Speech Was Printed

Later during the week, a newspaper - *The Inter Ocean, Chicago, Illinois · Tuesday, June 30, 1903* recorded that Rev. Thornton's words which some called inflammatory all white people were actually "pointed at the mob that roasted alive the negro White" The article titled **"How White Was Burned"** explained that people were upset because he hadn't had a trial and at the "barbarous cruelty of the men who took the law into their own hands."

How White Was Burned.

The Rev. M. W. Thornton, pastor of the First African Methodist Episcopal church of Wilmington, Del., said on Sunday night:

The white man, in the face of his boasted civilization, stands before my eyes tonight the demon of the world's races, a monster incarnate. He is a heathen, a fiend, a monstrosity before God. I would sooner trust myself in the den of a hyena than in the white man's arms.

This was pointed at the mob that roasted alive the negro White.

During the lynching when they had bound the accused George White with his hands tied behind his back, there was one man who made an "appeal for civilization", calling the mob to stop "for God's sake", preferring the mob just take his life instantly than torture him with being burned alive. The mob refused, repeating that the accused would be "burned alive".

After reading the full account, one can imagine the heightened terror, grief and anger in the area of

Wilmington, Delaware. Today, there is a plaque in Wilmington, Delaware in memory of Mr. George White and the lynching as a result of being only accused of murdering a white lady a week before. Meanwhile, the First A.M.E. Church to which Reverend M.W. Thornton was a pastor exonerated their pastor of any wrong doing in his speech.

The church also concluded that Thornton didn't incite Black Americans to riot or condemn white men as a whole, nor did he ask them to become outlaws by using Tracy tactics.

They believed that their pastor took a strong stance for justice along with true law and order during the entire

> The following, which also has a bearing on the White lynching, was given out for publication yesterday:
>
> Whereas, We the Official Board of Bethel A. M. E. Church in respect to the dignity of our institution, and that for which she stands in every moral crisis.
>
> Whereas, We appreciate the high and conservative stand taken by our beloved pastor, Rev. M. W. Thornton, D. D., in his manly stand for justice, law and order.
>
> Whereas, Insinuating resolutions have been passed by a negro church, reflecting on our body, and sayings of our pastor never uttered.
>
> Resolved, That we exonerate the Rev. M. W. Thornton, D. D ... any such aspersions and as a ... b express our confidence in him and his conservative remarks in the instance referred to.
>
> Resolved, That we regret the uncalled for and unkind resolutions of the church, that rushed so thoughtlessly with its condemnation on persons, on institutions of which they know little and whose cause they endeavored to place in a wrong light.
>
> Resolved, That the public should rightly understand, that Dr. Thornton uttered not a word "inciting his people to riot," "to outlaw Tracy tactics," or "condemnation of the white man as a whole," and each and every report published of the same, found its creation and expression in some other channel.
>
> Signed in behalf of church.
> Official Board.

ordeal. (Source: The Morning News, Wilmington, Delaware; Thu, Jul 9, 1903, Page 3)

As I, the editor, look back upon this history, I believe that if a government is being hypocritical, call it as such. If I was alive during a period such as the time of this lynching, self defense would have been the option to take when and if mobs came to take Black lives like the Knights of the White Shield were called to do – exterminate the Negro race.

I believe, just as in the days of Ester of the Bible when there is an execution order against an innocent people, God, just like He granted the Jews, through the king, the right of self defense and destroy all that came after them, He also expects and allows self defense before allowing those He loves to perish. One can even read in the Word of God when King David had to choose his punishment, he preferred being punished by God than by mankind because the latter has no mercy (2 Samuel 24:14). Those lynchmen had no mercy.

And lastly there is even the true law and order, and the Bible speaks on the laws of the land and that they should be just. It was unjust for people to be lynched solely because a mob accused due to the fact that it could have been an innocent man. According to the law, one is to prove it. This is why Solomon when he judged cases, was wise enough to prove who was innocent and guilty prior to a judgement, using the example of the baby whom he ordered to be cut in half in order to only determine who the true mother was. The true mother relinquished her rights to the child to spare it, thus, proving that she was the true biological mother. The other woman didn't mind at all if the baby was split in two or not.

It is through trial that one is to be found guilty, but if ever by mob, one will see clearly injustice, as this was what was handed down to Jesus the Christ Himself. For this was also mob's version of justice which was really injustice as they preferred to destroy Jesus Who did no wrong at all against a violent mob who decided him guilty while the true criminal they wanted set free.

This goes to provide evidence that in the 1800s in the United States of America, the sadistic racism of the times preferred the injustice in murdering someone not proven guilty, especially if he or she was a black person. No one stood up for fair trials for black people, especially right after black people were just emancipated fifty or so years prior, when they had absolutely no rights to even bring a case against a white man, and if it ever happened, most would sorely lose.

As for the case of Reverend M.W. Thornton, I conclude that he was a man like any man, and a preacher like many. The Bible states that even they will make mistakes at times (James 3:1-2, Romans 3:23 and Proverbs 24:16) as they are mere men, for not a one can bear the scars exactly like Jesus and there is only one purely good and that is God.

The Lord knows all men in whole, not solely in part. Therefore, may the true final judgements of all men rest in His hands – for the innocent and the guilty.

In conclusion, as pureness of heart is often referred to by the color white, Thornton gave his thoughts on this in the beginning of this manuscript, and how despite being called white, the actions of white Americans of his day were not white at all as in pure, but very dark, or evil. This goes to prove that when in relation to *racial* aspects, the words white and black don't carry the meanings pure or evil, respectively. *White means pure in the context of action only, and dark means evil in action only.* There are several Black men and women who are whiter than any racially white man if in fact that context means of pure and upstanding actions, and there are an immense number of racially white men and women who are as dark as night when it comes to their evil actions, darker than any racially Black man on earth.

Reverend Thornton went on to prove such in his manuscript – *The White Negro* or *A Series of Lectures on the Race Problem*.

–MIRIKA MAYO CORNELIUS